Due Return Date Date	Due Return Date Date

THE COMMUNIST POWER SYSTEM

THE  COMMUNIST POWER SYSTEM

Ota Šik

Translated by
Marianne Grund Freidberg

PRAEGER

PRAEGER SPECIAL STUDIES • PRAEGER SCIENTIFIC

Library of Congress Cataloging in Publication Data

Šik, Ota, 1919-
   The communist power system.

   Translation of Das kommunistische Machtsystem.
   Includes index.
   1. Communist state. 2. Russia--Politics and
government--1917-   3. Bureaucracy. 4. Europe,
Eastern--Politics and government. I. Title.
JC474.S4913 1980   321.9'2   80-22011
ISBN 0-03-044106-4

Published in 1981 by Praeger Publishers
CBS Educational and Professional Publishing
A Division of CBS, Inc.
521 Fifth Avenue, New York, New York 10175 U.S.A.

© Hoffmann und Campe Verlag, 1976
English translation © Hoffmann und Campe Verlag, 1981

123456789   145   987654321

Printed in the United States of America

PREFACE TO THE ENGLISH-LANGUAGE EDITION

Five years have passed since this book was written and first published in Germany. During these years, the communist power system in the East European countries has not changed essentially and its characteristic traits are still the same as described in the previous edition of this book. It is therefore not necessary to modify the original text for the English-language edition.

Although the system has remained the same, the economic and political situation has deteriorated as far as large segments of the population are concerned. In most Eastern European countries, labor productivity has slowed down and capital productivity has decreased. The economy is less efficient than before. But because the defense budget has continued to increase, the population is suffering the consequences in the form of still more shortages and a standard of living that compares even less favorably with the West than in the past. It is obvious even to the leading party bureaucrats that this "socialist" development has not inspired much enthusiasm in their people.

Within the ruling communist class in the Soviet Union as well as in the other Eastern European countries, the political insecurity has grown as a reaction to both the domestic economic and political situation, and the growing criticism from foreign socialist and communist quarters. This insecurity, together with the fear of liberalizing tendencies and their possible impact in the light of the Czechoslovakian experience, has led to a strengthening of neo-Stalinist positions, especially within the *Soviet* communist power structure. Consequently, in the late 1970s the political influence and position of pragmatic forces was further restricted.

The neo-Stalinist development finds its expression in a policy of intensified persecution and repression of all dissident movements within the country, and in an even more aggressive expansion of Soviet imperialist influence abroad. Soviet foreign policy is encouraged in its design by the unresolved or growing economic and social problems in the developing countries where it leads to political radicalization and to the foundation of Moscow-dominated, Marxist-revolutionary movements. This development more or less validates the Leninist theory of "revolutionary expansion of socialism to the weaker links of the capitalist-imperialist world chain" while supply-ing the political basis for the neo-Stalinist position. The neo-Stalinist strategy typical of Soviet policy of the 1970s and beginning of the 1980s has three characteristic traits: a strengthening of state power and the relentless repression of "antisocialist" trends at home; the expansion of the Moscow-dominated "socialist" sphere of influ-ence to all capitalist fault lines by means of military presence; and the definition of the final goal as the ultimate victory of "socialism" at world level.

I will try to demonstrate in this book that this development only serves to intensify a vicious circle that cannot be broken by Stalinist strategies. Rather, it will eventually promote anti-Stalinist forces that one day will overcome this so-called socialism. A strengthening of state and military power will have to be achieved at the expense of the population's standard of living. The priority given to heavy industry and military production will result necessarily in increased shortages of consumer goods production and services. This, in turn, will lead to the people's growing dissatisfaction with the economic and political situation, and it will stimulate demands for change and for reforms. In the long run, the Stalinist reaction in the form of increased repression at home and accelerated expansion abroad will create growing counterpressure that eventually will force the vicious circle of repression to give at its point of least resistance.

It is my absolute conviction that at some point in the future a humane and democratic reform will successfully be carried out in the Eastern European countries if the democratic forces in the entire world will be able to stop the neo-Stalinist imperialist advance by devising new solutions to the great economic and social problems in the developing countries, and by maintaining world peace. Demo-cratic socialism is a realistic alternative to both the present commu-nist system and to capitalism. It proposes a new approach to solving the immense socioeconomic problems of the future and to ensuring a more humane destiny for mankind. I am aware of the fact that socialist concepts meet with less understanding in the United States than in Western Europe, and that for this reason prejudices are very strong on the issue of democratic-socialist reform. There is a ten-dency to think in terms of "either . . . or," and any "noncapitalist" way of thinking is immediately termed "communist." I do hope that this book nevertheless will find enough readers who are interested in a criticism of the communist system even though this criticism originates from the position of democratic socialism.

It should be stressed here that the definition of democratic socialism includes the concept of a system that has nothing in common with socialism as practiced today in the Eastern European countries. The new concept is based on different principles, which I have recently explained in detail in my book *Humane Economic Democracy* (Hamburg, 1979). An economic and social order of this kind would include the indispensable and positive features of private enterprise and of a market mechanism, and at the same time would overcome the threatening economic alienation of large segments of the population as well as the capitalist system's lack of vision for the future. It is, in fact, a social theory suggesting the realistic possibility of a Third Way.

In the past, conditions in Czechoslovakia had been favorable enough for a Third Way to become reality. In the future, conditions in the Soviet Union and in other countries will be similarly favorable. The underlying concepts have been formulated on the basis of the experience with, and analysis of, the shortcomings of both systems. Therefore, they should provide the answer to the increasing questions asked by large segments of the population everywhere in the world on the future structure of society.

In the Soviet state-monopolistic system as well as in the Western capitalist countries, the bureaucratization of society has to be considered the greatest threat to mankind. For this very reason, the following analysis of the phenomenon of bureaucratization as well as the search for an antibureaucratic development toward democracy are of utmost importance. The bureaucratization of Soviet society cannot be dismissed as just an Asian phenomenon. This trend is related to very strong tendencies toward concentration and to unresolved growth explosions. It therefore constitutes a real threat to the Western industrial nations as well. By attempting to differentiate between the general substance of bureaucratic power on the one hand and the specifically Soviet bureaucratic mechanism on the other hand, this book will stimulate the reader to give serious thought to this very pressing issue.

Ota Šik
St. Gallen, Switzerland

CONTENTS

THE COMMUNIST POWER SYSTEM

INTRODUCTION

The social order introduced in the Soviet Union by the Communist Party of Russia (Bolsheviks) after the October Revolution and adopted after World War II under Soviet influence or direct political pressure in many other countries is generally called a socialist system. In reference to Marxist-Leninist theory, the nature of this system is described as "socialist" by the Communist Parties in the countries within the Soviet sphere of influence, i.e., the communist countries of Eastern Europe. This theory is used not only to prove the socialist content of the existing system, but also to discredit any attempts at introducing essential reforms of the system by democratic socialists as "antisocialist," "counterrevolutionary" tendencies. In other words, it is claimed that the existing system basically corresponds to the theoretical concept of socialism as formulated by Marx, Engels, and Lenin, and that these theories have irrevocably outlined the necessary and essential traits of a socialist order of society. Therefore, anyone who proposes to change the system by eliminating some of its typical features would be an anti-Marxist and antisocialist. This view and argumentation is unscientific and dogmatic, and serves to conceal important facts that are in contradiction to the "evidence of socialism" for the following reasons.

First, certain features of the system are described as "socialist principles" (state property of the means of production, centralized economic planning, political power in the hands of the Communist Party, and so forth) without investigating whether these principles really correspond to the interests of the workers. There is no possibility of analyzing the system's social and political structure, or the relationship between the decision-making process of political organs on the one hand and the interests of the majority of the population on the other hand. In this way, the system's antisocialist power structure remains concealed by superficial pseudosocialist traits.

Second, verbal references to the theories of Marx, Engels, and Lenin are related to a one-sided and biased interpretation of these theories aimed at masking the system's antisocialist nature. The classic theories are primarily used to provide justification for such features as the dictatorship of the proletariat exercised by the Communist Party, the socialization of the means of production by way of nationalization, centralized economic planning in the form of dirigistic plans, and so forth. However, the essential demands made by Marx and Engels upon a socialist society are either ignored or dismissed on the ground that they "cannot be realized yet" or are "a future goal," such as the liberation of the worker from political repression and the systematic, gradual liquidation of the bureaucratic state in the course of communist development, the elimination of any form of exploitation of the productive workers and their direct participation in decisions concerning the development of labor and use of the results of labor, the end of the workers' alienation from their place of work, from the enterprises, from the economic base, from the administrative organs, and so forth.

Third, the theories of Marx, Engels, and Lenin are treated as eternal truths, but the decisive criterion of any scientific approach as stressed by Marx and Lenin themselves is neglected, namely, the concurrence of theory and reality, the theory's evaluation in practice, and its continuous adjustment on the basis of practical experience. Marxist-Leninist theory is not confronted with reality. It is not assessed in the light of new experience and knowledge. Many simplified or erroneous assumptions remain concealed. Thus, it becomes almost impossible to eliminate critically the theoretical concept of economic planning replacing the market mechanism that has proved too simplistic and immensely wasteful for society. The most detrimental theoretical inadequacy is the lack of provisions for solving problems such as conflicting interests within a socialist society, the absolute rule by a bureaucracy, the nonexistent criterion of effectivity, or insufficient interest by the producer in an optimal economic development.[1] These shortcomings must not be exposed, and certainly not theoretically corrected, as long as the new theory would oppose the interests of the ruling bureaucracy. In the Eastern European countries, the Marxist-Leninist theory has thus become a state religion serving to support an antisocialist system. Therefore, references to the Marxist-Leninist theory are no evidence of the fact that the system existing in the Soviet Union and within its sphere of influence is indeed a genuinely socialist system.

In the following chapters, I will demonstrate why this system is *not a socialist system*. It should become quite clear that the essential demands put upon a socialist society (upon the first stage of a communist society) contained in Marx's theory [2] have not been met in the system now existing in the Eastern European countries. However, guidelines for a socialist society cannot be established only on the basis of Marx's theory; they have to be complemented and concretized in the light of practical experience.

Without having to digress from Marx's fundamental requirements, I want to describe the system's major obstacles and shortcomings that forestall the implementation of Marx's basic requirements, obstacles which he did not foresee and which are not specifically mentioned in the official Marxist-Leninist literature as accepted and propagated by Communist Parties. These basic shortcomings have to be eliminated if the existing system is to be transformed into a truly socialist system. Consequently, another essential obligation of socialist society is to analyze theoretically the system's shortcomings and to demonstrate convincingly the ways and means of dealing with these shortcomings.

The communist system's most detrimental trait and major obstacle to introducing genuine socialism has to be seen in the *absolute rule of a specific bureaucracy*. The origins and the specific structure of this bureaucracy and the mechanism of its power structure will be described on the basis of both theoretical analysis and many years of personal experience. At the same time it will become clear that the most essential condition for eliminating bureaucratic domination, and thus for establishing a socialist society, is the development of *democratic conditions*. There can be no socialism without democracy. Without democracy, there will be no socialist freedom for the working individual; without democratic conditions, the new and ever-expanding bureaucracy will invariably evolve into a new ruling class commanding unlimited means of repression. Under democratic conditions, all the shortcomings in the economic area, in the cultural development, and so forth would have been eliminated a long time ago, whereas without democracy they have become insolvable and conducive to even further bureaucratic deformation and repression.

From the point of view of democratic socialism, the system currently existing in the Eastern European countries cannot be termed a socialist system. I feel justified to call this system a *communist system* for the name of the political parties that have established this system. However, this term must not lead to identifying the system with Marx's and Engels' concept of communism, or any other communist utopia. A communist system is one that has been established in the countries of Eastern Europe on the basis of the exclusive seizure of power by historically evolved Communist Parties and is wrongly called a socialist system by the official party and state ideology. The term "communist system" as such does not express the decisively dominating nature of the system. Therefore, the adjectives "party-bureaucratic" or "state-monopolistic" describe the system more accurately; the first choice alludes to the specifically bureaucratic feature of its power structure, the second to the most characteristic trait of its economy.

This terminology does not by any means describe the real nature of the system, but it helps one understand some of its major features—the bureaucratic power structure and the state-monopolistic economic structure. These will be described in detail later. The chapter on the origins of the Soviet bureaucratic system will highlight those stages in the development of the system that illustrate the theoretical vagueness in the issue of "market relations in a socialist economy" and its practical implications, as well as those that demonstrate the fact that the nonunderstanding of the bureaucratic problem, of the theoretical gap, has largely contributed to the bureucratization of the system. Finally, it is intended to substantiate with historical evidence the contention that in the Soviet Union, as later in all countries within the communist system, all major changes in party leadership politics had to correspond to the interests of the party bureaucracy. This implies that not the party itself and certainly not the working class but the established party bureaucracy has the final decision in matters of party leadership and its politics. Since this is true for all Eastern European countries despite differing social structures, I chose the example of the Soviet Union's political development and its most decisive political events in order to illustrate the communist power mechanism common to all these countries.

It is therefore not my intention to present a complex historical study of Soviet political development, but to demonstrate the *decisive* interrelationship of party bureaucracy, party leadership, and party and state politics—connections which in the existing historical works tend to disappear all too often in the great mass of detailed and superficial information. One is often inclined to attribute the decisive influence on communist politics to one of the leading personalities without perceiving the party apparatus as the power behind the scene. But even historians looking to explain the makeup of a specific party leadership or policy by the given internal and external political and economic circumstances tend to neglect the specific interest of the party bureaucracy that may change with the circumstances but still remain the decisive element.

The fact that the party bureaucracy's influence on the development of the communist system is not clearly perceived is mostly due to the insufficient attention given to the specific position of the party bureaucracy in a communist system, and to the lack of understanding of the mechanism that serves to promote the bureaucracy's power and interests. The analysis of the nature of the communist bureaucracy and of its power mechanism will demonstrate why and how the bureaucracy acceeds to absolute power within a communist system. It is exclusively due to this bureaucratic power that perfectly realistic humane and socialist concepts have been perverted in communist practice to such an extent that for innumerable workers in Eastern Europe, as well as abroad, the term socialism has become a symbol of totalitarian repression. The present analysis purports to furnish the evidence that it is not socialism but communist bureaucratism that has created suppression.

NOTES

1. Ota Šik, *The Third Way—Marxist-Leninist Theory and Modern Industrial Society* (London-New York, 1976).
2. Ibid., p. 375.

1

ORIGINS AND DEVELOPMENT OF THE SOVIET BUREAUCRATIC SYSTEM

IDEOLOGICAL PREMISES

The history of Russia after the October Revolution was determined primarily by two factors: the economic backwardness of the country, characterized by predominantly small-scale agricultural and handicraft production with only a negligible number of industrial enterprises; and the theoretical concepts of the Bolshevik leadership, which had a decisive influence on the structure of the new state and the overall social restructuring. The prewar economy of the Russian empire had reached a level of development that required extensive market relations. Although a number of more or less self-sustaining, backward settlements in very remote regions could exist without regular market relations on the basis of a simple barter economy, the medium-sized villages and, of course, the cities were dependent on the trade of a large class of private merchants. Due to rapid inflation and an appalling shortage of goods during the war, trade increasingly took on the character of barter—exchange of goods for goods. A mounting wave of speculation flooded the entire country.

It was only after the communist seizure of power that systematic revolutionary changes were initiated which necessarily and essentially reflected the theoretical concepts of the communist leadership. A centralized economic management was to dictate the most important lines of production and distribution on the basis of a modernized and highly concentrated industrial production and establish a direct link between production and consumption without the intermediary of a market.

Lenin had been deeply impressed by the state capitalist war economy in Germany and especially by the state-controlled production and distribution system. To Lenin, state capitalism, the overall control of production and distribution by the state, seemed to be one possible form of transition to socialist production and direct distribution without a market structure. Consequently, the initial economic measures were designed to put these concepts into practice: socialization of the land, forced syndicalism of the industry, nationalization of banks, private railroads, foreign trade, the merchant marine, and all large industrial plants, and, in 1920, of all businesses with more than five workers. Organized workers' control was gradually changed into a system of centralized economic state management. However, the central control organs were keen on supervising not only overall industrial production but also the distribution of the means of production and of the labor force. The distribution of grain by the state became especially important: The so-called "grain monopoly" at first involved official grain purchases by the state, then confiscations and requisitions, still later state-controlled exchanges of industrial goods for agrarian products, and, finally, government allocations of consumer goods to the population.

The tendency toward achieving direct state control of the entire socialist production process and a distribution system without a market, as well as universal accounting and control of all nonsocialist production and distribution (in view of their gradual integration into the socialist power structure) unequivocally reflected the original theories of socialist economy. It was a systematic attempt at eliminating a free market, which Lenin viewed as a capitalist institution or, at least, as a process leading to capitalism. An ideal starting point was the large class of small-scale producers, especially peasants, whose innate preference for capitalism was, according to Lenin's view at the time, to be eliminated by government accounting and control of all distribution systems.[1] It would therefore be a mistake to assume that the policies aimed at eliminating a free market and at introducing a system of direct distribution were determined exclusively by the difficult economic situation during the war and postwar years. The wartime system of rationing undoubtedly favored the tendency toward establishing a network of direct distribution throughout the country, and theoretically there was no doubt at this stage that this was the appropriate political course to take. However, the theory of immediate socialization bypassing the stage of market economy had already been clearly exposed in Lenin's draft for the party program submitted in March 1918 to the Seventh Party Congress of the Russian Communist Party (of Bolsheviks): "In the area of distribution it is the present task of the Soviet regime to continue its efforts to replace trade by a systematic state-wide organized distribution of products. The entire population has to be organized in production and consumption collectives capable of distributing, on the basis of strict centralization of the entire distribution apparatus, all necessary products as rapidly and economically as possible, with a minimum of labor involved."[2]

There is already evidence here of serious theoretical simplifications indicating that the underlying causes for the vital existence of a market—even in socialist ownership systems—were being ignored, although objectively these causes could not be removed. Lenin was aware of some of these simplifications and he tried to initiate practical changes. However, he was unable to foresee the effect of some others since they were not part of his personal experience but surfaced only later in the course of the country's industrial development.

There was one negative and highly consequential trait in Lenin's personality, as in all of his successors and of most leaders in the communist movement: he was extremely authoritarian and unyielding when putting to practice certain theoretical concepts in which he firmly believed. Lenin's own remarkable theoretical and polemic talent convinced him time and again that the goals which he had set were the absolute correct ones; it also reinforced his harsh, even unmitigated reaction to any oppositional view. Lenin's revolutionary purposiveness was backed by an incredibly strong will and, in contrast to his successors, it was certainly "the cause" and not personal power that mattered to him.[3] Lenin's almost fanatical revolutionary drive to obtain the "obvious necessities" was the source of his intolerance, which made him neglect even justified criticism and opposing ideas. Doubts concerning Russia's revolutionary development were in most instances harshly refuted by Lenin, even when voiced in socialist circles. After the seizure of power Lenin rashly discarded the ideas of his theoretical opponents as pronouncements of the class enemy, although these ideas often contained suggestions for alternative ways and means of establishing a socialist society for which there existed at the time only insufficiently evaluated and debated theories as to its form and organization.[4]

The subject involved was not some insignificant experiment but the reconstruction of an entire social order deciding the fate of millions of people (and, indirectly, of humanity as a whole). Therefore, Lenin's other personality trait, positive this time, of publicly admitting and subsequently correcting mistakes and erroneous conclusions, was not sufficient as a counterbalance to his own "revolutionary impatience."[5] It was not until later under Lenin's successors (who lacked not only his theoretical talent but also his courage to openly confess to mistakes and political changes) that intolerance toward differing opinions, ideas, and concepts along with the rigorous application of simplified and outdated theories became such a disastrous characteristic of communist leadership.

In the beginnings of the "socialist reconstruction" Lenin applied, or proposed to apply, the following essential theoretical simplifications:

1. The concept of market-free supply and centralization of agricultural products by private peasants and a state-controlled distribution of these products, distribution of industrial goods to the countryside, and elimination of money;[6]

2. The idea of a general labor service obligation (even for smallholder peasants) and of a centrally controlled allocation of work to all persons capable of work;[7]

3. The theory that industrial enterprises would be able, with the assistance of centralized state organs and in the absence of a market, to ensure the production required by society;

4. The conception that a bureaucratization of the central administrative structure would be a necessary evil in view of Russia's low cultural standard which could be raised only by improving general education and by extending state control.[8]

Practical experience, however, led Lenin very soon to recognize that the first two of these theoretical concepts were erroneous. He openly admitted his mistakes and initiated radical changes in the entire economic structure. But he never became aware of the fact that the last two concepts were equally false. It is these last two, though, which are still being followed today although their grave social consequences should have been recognized a long time ago. The fact that they are still being applied today is, however, not a problem of recognition but a matter of stubborn conservation of evidently false premises. This situation is the logical outcome of the existent bureaucratic power structures.

The Bolshevik leadership with Lenin as its head was forced to recognize above all the necessity of market relations with the small peasant villages.[9] The peasants could not be made to comply with their delivery obligations, neither in the form of voluntary levies nor by way of forced requisitions. In fact, it turned out that a barter economy (trading in kind) meant a step backward compared to a money economy since trading in kind did not provide the peasant with sufficient choices for individual and independent purchases and thus removed the incentive to produce. Therefore, the state agencies were forced to go back to purchasing agricultural products in exchange for money, leaving the farmer free to buy the industrial goods of his own choice. Money circulation thus proved to be a precondition for any future increase of agricultural as well as industrial production.[10]

The transition to the New Economic Policy (NEP) in 1921 was the practical application of the theoretical insight that the economical needs of society cannot be satisfied by way of direct government distribution of products or by means of labor service obligation instead of a direct exchange of products between city and countryside, the Soviet government now encouraged the development of a market economy regulated by money. This policy even led to the use of real money paralleled by a fight against inflation, as well as to the introduction of a currency convertible into gold to be used in international transactions (zolotyj tscherwonec).

Lenin equally realized the disadvantages of a general labor service obligation and the impossibility of creating initiative through labor controls and moral incentives. Labor service does not stimulate interest in the evolution of a given work process, and it is not at all inducive to improving qualifications or to encouraging job changes. Only voluntary labor—and this includes free acceptance or refusal of work—on the basis of human self-interest can encourage individual initiative for work. Lenin therefore began stressing not only the importance of material reward in the form of money but also the priority of this material incentive (as opposed to ethical) during a historically extended phase of development of the socialist society.[11]

The fact that chozrastschot (cost accounting in the enterprises) is stressed as important implies the understanding that entire enterprise collectives should strive for maximum profitability. But then Lenin did not draw the conclusion that production cannot actually be determined by central administrative bodies and that, in the absence of market conditions, chozrastschot alone does not encourage an enterprise to achieve the most efficient or socially appropriate production.

Although Lenin repeatedly stressed the importance of controlling the measure of labor and consumption,[12] he was not sufficiently aware of the incredibly complicated concept of "labor." In its universal, quantitatively and qualitatively required social development, labor cannot be centrally planned and controlled by any administration. Probably Lenin's most essential error was that he greatly underestimated self-interest and initiative of enterprise collectives in the development of the technical, economical, and qualitative aspects of production and its microstructural flexibility. He failed to conceive of the positive influence of market pressure on enterprise efficiency and its irreplaceability as the essential factor for the objective application of subjective production decisions in the individual socialist enterprise over a relatively long period of social development. Of course, at the time nobody had had sufficient experience in developing socialist industrial production, and Lenin was all too caught up in theoretical concepts exploring various possibilities for governing a socialist state. He therefore considered the reintroduction of a market solely as a temporary concession to Russia's petty-bourgeois (peasant) character, dispensable in a future, fully socialized production system. To have overestimated the government's administrative possibilities and qualifications; not to have understood the necessity of a market even in an entirely socialized production system; and, above all, not to have been able to conceive of the causes of a specific bureaucratization of state and party as a consequence of the complete centralization and monopolization of power and of the gradual elimination of democratic principles from political life were indeed grave errors of judgment that were to have a fateful influence on the future social development.

Although Lenin during the last years of his life was greatly appalled by the rapidly growing state and party bureaucracy,[13] he was not able to see the relationship between this phenomenon and the highly centralized and monopolistic political system that he himself had helped create. Instead, he blamed this development on the petty-bourgeois mentality of the majority of the Russian people and on their cultural backwardness. Consequently, Lenin called for long-term educational efforts and an extension of the Workers' and Peasants' Inspection and Control as the most efficient remedies for improving this situation. He did not live long enough to find out that even in highly culturally and industrially developed countries bureaucratization occurs automatically with the introduction of similarly monopolistic political power systems, and that no amount of control, however broadly based, can prevent such a development.

THE PROCESS OF BUREAUCRATIZATION

As the system's defenders are invariably pointing out, there were definite reasons for an initial centralization of the postrevolutionary state administration in Russia. However, the attempt alone of solving objective problems by a centralized decision-making process is proof enough of simplified concepts of planning and control as well as of an excessive claim for power by the party. The long-accepted doctrine that only the Communist Party would be able to recognize and represent the interests of the workers had led to exaggerated distrust in any opposing views, to their increasingly violent suppression, and finally—under Stalin—to mass terror. The beginnings of this development, however, had already become obvious during Lenin's leadership.

Having been economically disrupted by the war and the civil war, Russia initially lacked everything it needed: consumer goods, raw materials, foodstuffs, transportation, and so forth so that only a state distribution system could bring rapid relief. The work ethic had greatly deteriorated not only during the long years of war but also because of wrongly interpreted revolutionary achievements. This called for stricter work control and a systematic fight against economic irresponsibility that was particularly obvious in the case of the revolutionary collective administrations (obezlitschka).[14]

The lack of specialists was particularly disastrous. Industrially and culturally a backward country, Russia had few economic and technical experts to begin with, and these were mostly members of the old ruling classes. Therefore, these people did not have the confidence of the workers. Classified as counterrevolutionary elements, they had mostly been dismissed from their jobs if they had not yet left the country on their own initiative.

This situation was very favorable to an overall development toward concentration and centralization which, backed up by simplified theoretical assumptions, easily met with approval by zealous proponents. The lack of dependable administrators in the lower-level production management organs, the impractical concepts of one-person directorship, the primitive "principle of democratic centralism," and the lack of means of production all gradually reinforced the position of the vast upper-echelon central administrative apparatus, which was responsible for distributing the means of production, for allocating labor and financial funds, and for setting production goals. Also, it filled the posts in the lower-level economic administrations, and supervised and controlled the activities and achievements of these officials.

Such increasing concentration of economic management in the upper-level organs together with a growing centralization of the "final decisions" in the party apparatus inevitably led to a rapidly expanding bureaucracy. The lack of objective and subjective conditions for establishing a complex and comprehensive administration and the incapability of many officials to understand increasingly complicated economic mechanisms and to cope with an overwhelming amount of information and regulations necessitated more division of labor within each sphere of activities. The resulting breakup of administrative tasks into various subfunctions and the fact that quantity replaced quality made it even more difficult to supervise and efficiently coordinate individual activities. The original idea and content of leadership tasks gradually disappeared while administrating became an end in itself.[15] The various divisions of the apparatus were operating separately, which inevitably caused duplication of work and red tape, a growing isolation of the bureaucratic machine, increasing inefficiency, and incalculable costs.[16]

As the state apparatus steadily expanded and more and more nonparty officials had to be employed, and as public criticism of bureaucratism in the state organs became more vocal, the Communist Party increased its efforts to gain control over the state's bureaucracy. Bureaucratism was blamed on enemy activities of noncommunist or even counterrevolutionary officials, the remedy sought in stricter controls by the party. This, however, meant nothing other than expanding the party apparatus that was supposed to control the political and economic administration. Each government department, every public organization was supervised by special sections of the central and regional party apparatus. This, in turn, immensely swelled the party machine, expanded and complicated its range of functions, and slowly transformed party officials recruited among the politically most trusted communists into bureaucrats. Thus a superbureaucracy developed within the regular government bureaucracy.

Simultaneously, there was the development of specifically bureaucratic interests. The party apparatus, wielding power by filling all subordinate jobs, decided on the material well-being and professional future of many people as well as on the allocation of vital goods, while abusive and arbitrary decisions were hard to prove. These features explain why, to many people, joining the party bureaucracy seemed socially important and attractive. There was struggle within the apparatus for higher positions, which resulted almost automatically in a further swelling. New departments and sections were created—and more jobs became available.

Soon after the revolution there was strong opposition among the workers against the increasing bureaucratization of state and party leadership. The Workers' Opposition grouped communists as well as noncommunists and before long held all key positions in the trade unions. The workers very soon became aware of the fact that the bureaucratic apparatus was far removed from real life, that it was characterized by schematism and rigidity, by internal contradictions and divisional limitations, by useless or abusive orders and regulations. The workers increasingly recognized that in fact the bureaucracy functioned in opposition to the workers' own interests and that it became practically impossible to promote their own interests against those of the administrative apparatus and of the political power organs.

Above all, the workers learned by experience that there was no recourse in criticism of bureaucratic orders and actions, and that the workers lacked the necessary information and specific knowledge as well as an understanding for existing interrelations. It became obvious that politicians and bureaucrats worked hand in hand and had ways and means of silencing their critics, and that the majority of those occupying powerful positions had not really been elected but appointed by a higher-placed power apparatus. Therefore, the antibureaucratic opposition urged a democratization of the leadership in the form of collective management of enterprises and of all top-level economic organs.[17]

Although Lenin in his draft of the party program in 1918 had suggested that workers' organizations (trade unions, workers' councils, and so forth) become the controlling organs of the socialist production organization,[18] he gradually changed his opinion of such collegiate authorities. Above all, Lenin distrusted the workers' councils which, he felt, increasingly opposed the tutelage of the workers by the Communist Party apparatus and by the centralized bureaucratic administration of the national economy. Also, more and more noncommunists were elected to the workers' councils. Thus, in 1919 Lenin attempted to replace the workers' councils with trade unions that would then be responsible for passing the state organ's decisions on to the workers.[19]

Lenin and even more so Trotsky consistently pursued a policy of militarizing the production management. Enterprises were to be assigned certain production targets and the individual workers certain tasks. In the interest of increasing productivity and in order to overcome the economic crisis, these "assignments" were to take the form of military orders passed along from the highest to the lowest level, from the state economic organ to the responsible director and down to the individual worker. The direct worker democracy was to be replaced by a disciplined and hierarchically organized command organization reaching from the highest state authority down to each enterprise.[20] In such a setup, the trade union would be a mass organization of the workers designed to support the activities of the commanding state organ by convincing the working masses of the social necessity of state management and by supervising efficiency and productivity. The resulting shift in the union's function from defending the workers' immediate interests concerning wages and working conditions to organizing production lines, promoting the achievement of production targets, and controlling the work process was the reason for the increasing bureaucratization of the trade unions themselves.

Furthermore, there was the question whether production management in the enterprise should be entrusted to elected trade union organs, or to state-nominated directors. While Lenin stressed the necessity of nominating directly responsible directors as opposed to the "democratic centralism" of collegiate bodies and, therefore, did not envisage replacing the workers' councils with new collegiate trade union organs, the Workers' Opposition represented by Shliapnikov, who was also a member of the party's Central Committee, was trying to maintain the collective production management by union councils. The Workers' Opposition was the expression of the strong antibureaucratic attitude of the workers as well as of all those among the intellectuals who were fighting for a democratization of the system. The unions were not only to plan and control production in the enterprises but, through elected interenterprise organs with an elected central economic body at the top, they were to plan and control the entire national economy. This was a fight for overall economic democratization and economic self-management of the workers.

Lenin viewed the Workers' Opposition as a threat to the socialist revolution for it challenged his conviction that only a strict state organization under the leadership of the Communist Party would ensure an economic development in the interest of the workers. All functionaries not selected and nominated by the party might serve as a front for unreliable or even antisocialist elements. Therefore, the proposals submitted by the Workers' Opposition had to be attacked and suppressed. From late 1920 to Spring of 1921, the party intensively discussed this issue until Lenin, supported mainly by Zinoviev, eventually defeated the Workers' Opposition. This outcome was due partly to Lenin's personality but also to the active support of the party apparatus, which in so doing defended its own interests. It is certain that Lenin's arguments did not correspond to the long-term interests of the workers.

In the discussion of this issue, both the unions (in formulating their demand for collective administration) and the party leadership, especially Lenin himself, confused two different processes between which it is extremely important to differentiate even though they are closely linked: first, the organization of the actual operative management of the production process and, second, the democratic supervision and control of management as well as the selection of the people in charge of management.

To the outside, the discussion centered on the issue of collective management versus management by a few individuals. The union representatives kept stressing the importance of democratic, that is, collective, management and of administrative organs down to the individual enterprise, meaning not so much to reject the concept of operative management by individuals as to have these individuals placed under the control of democratically elected collective organs.[21] Lenin, however, argued exclusively in favor of "one man leadership." He underlined the necessity of production management by one highly qualified and technically experienced director while criticizing the irresponsibility of collegiate bodies and the replacement of an expert management by mechanical administration.[22]

There was and there is no doubt about the fact that production management by one director has definite advantages over collective management. It was therefore hardly possible at the time to come up with a valid counterargument. Lenin's view could hardly be refuted that the coordination of production, transportation, and so forth called for one responsible and determined person while collective management would lead to irresponsibility and undecidedness.[23] However, already at his time and repeatedly in later years, this was not the central issue. The problem was to decide who should select, nominate, supervise, and, if necessary, dismiss the director, to whom the managing directors should report, and who should represent the workers' interests within the enterprise. It was not the concept of "one-man management" colliding with the idea of "collective management" but the proponents of "a leading role of the party" opposing the advocates of an "antibureaucratic and democratic self-government of the workers."[24]

However, the identification of an operative production management that doubtlessly requires qualified specialists with a collective self-government of the workers and its refusal as a "petty-bourgeois anarcho-syndicalist" tendency (a humiliating reproach ever since invoked against any attempt at introducing workers' councils) did not invalidate the justification of such self-management. Basic decisions concerning the long-term development of an enterprise and its development options, the long-term evaluation of management and its achievements, and the solution of conflicts between enterprise collective and management have to be made only occasionally and thus do not disrupt operative management. The same can be said of supervision and control. All these functions can and should be exercised by democratically elected collective organs.

During the period immediately after the revolution it was still justified to argue that the working class was not sufficiently educated for such basic decision making and controlling tasks. But after a few years of socialist development, this argument should have been discarded especially in view of the fact that workers and employees acquire the necessary knowledge and qualifications not only by theoretical training but also and mainly by practical experience. But in the course of those initial discussions it became obvious that the foremost reasons for suppressing democratically elected collective management organs had to be seen, first, in the political distrust toward the working classes and, second, in the overestimation of the intellectual maturity and moral integrity of the Communist Party. This misjudgment was linked to a fatal unawareness of the increasing bureaucratization of the party itself as a consequence of its monopolistic power position, as well as to a merciless suppression of all divergent political opinions and parties.[25]

Theoretically, this development resulted from the fact that existing conflicts of social interests were ignored, and that specifically bureaucratic and above all political interests were awakened in those who held positions of power and control. It is surprising that the Marxists who always and more than any others pointed to the function of antagonistic class interests should have underestimated to such an extent the specific interests and conflicts of interests within the population and especially between the ruling and the ruled. The reason very probably lies in the exclusive preoccupation with exactly these class conflicts. All social differentiations and conflicts of interests that did not relate to the antagonism between labor and capital were almost completely ignored.

This is not the only theoretically weak argumentation that has to be pointed out here. Equally important was the drive for power of the worker leadership, which exalted in its own "infallibility" and "authority" and which failed to perceive the conflicts arising between the masses and the power apparatus. These men projected their belief in the absolute correctness of their own convictions unto the party that they were leading. This is true to a great extent in the case of Lenin and it explains why he overestimated the "conscious" and "guiding" role of the Communist Party, his fanatical belief that this party alone would be capable of leading the workers, and that all democratically elected organs of workers or producers could only be antisocialist.[26]

Lenin ignored the workers' powerlessness against the vested interests of the bureaucracy, which were reflected in all important decisions and appointments characterizing the entire party apparatus—from state administration down to nominated directors, and made it immune from the workers' criticism. Although Lenin talked about the incredible bureaucratization of the party, he expected the same party to fight bureaucratism while at the same time denouncing as class enemies all those organizations and movements that represented the workers' demands. Lenin was no longer able and willing to see that in the process of suppressing all oppositional trends, the Communist Party functionaries became the main pillars of bureaucratic despotism and that, under the pretext of fighting the class enemy, these party officials in reality suppressed any criticism within the working class. Appeals to the party to try and overcome bureaucratism had the opposite effect and resulted in the further consolidation of the party apparatus' power. This development was also the end of the few "democratic" concepts of a socialist society that initially had existed at least in theory. At the same time the workers' collectives lost their interest in the development of the country's production potentials, which had been the major concern of the Workers' Opposition.[27]

UNDEMOCRATIC DEVELOPMENT

Any chance of introducing democratic institutions for the benefit of the working class as originally demanded by Lenin and included in his draft program for the Seventh Party Congress of the Russian Communist Party[28] had been exploited to obtain the opposite effect. It was the Communist Party that decided on possibilities for political manifestations for the people, on the formulation and application of the people's will, its ideas and wishes. Outside the party and apart from the party's opinions and dictates, there was no room for initiative by the people. Discussions, criticism, and suggestions, the election of representatives, and so forth were only possible with the consent and under the supervision of the party organs but never against their will. Any action undertaken by the workers that had not been approved by the party was interpreted as being antiparty and antisocialist and was therefore suppressed.

The idea in itself is unrealistic and undemocratic that the party as the only political institution would be able to recognize and express the incredibly wide range of actual human wishes, interests, ideas, and propositions, that one party can replace an entire people's political initiative. It means that the population has no possibilities to express different opinions than the ones decreed by the party organs, and that it cannot give its confidence to representatives other than those suggested or approved by the party. This is a blatant discrimination against the workers, and it means in practice that the majority of the people is being excluded from the political process, becoming a passive mass of manipulated and politically estranged citizens. At the same time, a small section of the population is entitled to privileges, which in itself is reason enough to engender conflict with the working classes.

Such a state of affairs cannot be condoned and accepted by the majority of the people because it symbolizes the contrast between politically privileged and unprivileged citizens, between the governing and the governed. To disagree with the party's actions or not to become a member of the party may lead to total exclusion from active political life or, at best, to being limited to a passive, "controlled" activity within the trade union or any other social organization. For this simple reason there could be no question of a "fuller democracy." Instead of a "democracy for the majority" a new *dictatorship of the minority over the majority* was established.

The oft-repeated theory that the "dictatorship of the bourgeoisie over the working classes as a dictatorship of the minority over the majority" would change into a "dictatorship of the proletariat, that is, a dictatorship of the working majority over the bourgeois minority" was historically wrong from the very beginning. In the practice of all "socialist states" it had led to "dictatorship of the bureaucratic power over the working people." Whenever the workers, dissatisfied with the actions of the communists, have turned to other mediators and representatives to help promote their own convictions and demands, they have been accused of supporting antisocialist elements or of planning counterrevolutionary actions.[29] Even though the workers swore allegiance to the socialist principles and promised to defend the socialist system, wanting only to cut down on the bureaucratic overhead and to eliminate the corrupted cadres who mostly justified their actions with party orders, and even though they only demanded secret democratic elections of representatives whom they could completely trust and who were not stamped by the bureaucratic apparatus,[30] such demands were invariably termed "counterrevolutionary" and, often violently, suppressed.[31]

After the Kronstadt rising, workers and peasants without any party affiliation tried many times and by different means to fend off the tutelage and bureaucratic dictate of the Communist Party cadres. There have been protests, demonstrations, and armed insurrections within the Soviet Union as well as among workers in Hungary, Poland, and Czechoslovakia. But there have never been any open discussions of the real causes for the resistance of the working classes, who as the theoretically ruling classes should find other ways of getting satisfaction. As in the case of Kronstadt, the official reason invariably has been the petty bourgeoisie and its discontent with the economic situation and especially the agitation of the foreign bourgeoisie.[32]

However, one fact has always been and is still being concealed: just as in Kronstadt, it was workers who in their speeches and proclamations expressed their powerlessness against the bureaucratic dictatorship while clearly disassociating themselves from capitalism and its representatives. Also, no one has ever been able to explain why the foreign bourgeoisie and the political emigrants should have had a stronger political influence on the working masses than the communists themselves, who after all were in a position to talk directly to the workers. It seems that it should have been possible to deal with disorder, difficulties, and shortcomings in ways that would have satisfied the working classes or, at least, discouraged rebellion. The fact that desperate actions occurred repeatedly must mean that the people no longer believed in the communist promises, that they mostly identified the communists with those bureaucrats responsible for the most horrendous mistakes, injustices, and abuses. However, any such accusation has always been rejected as unjustified.[33]

Generally, it was sufficient for the workers to express their distrust of communist functionaries, whose activities they had been able to closely observe to be branded "antisocialist." Above all, the communist leadership rejected any demand for democratic elections, arguing that the election of other than communist representatives would lead to the restoration of capitalism. But it failed to mention its fear that communist representatives may have lost in free elections. And it did not mention that this fear alone was a sign of bureaucratization and of the unpopularity of most of the communist functionaries who, having been nominated in the absence of a real elective process, had become alienated from the people and had lost their confidence.

The argument that the communists determined, expressed, and promoted the interests of the workers must be countered by stating that this was an entirely abstract proclamation without any guarantee for a genuine representation of popular interests. Such a guarantee is only given in the case where individuals claiming to represent a certain social group regularly and prior to any political decision have to be confirmed in their mandate by the group, report to it, and can be dismissed by it. Only in situations where social groups have a free choice among several candidates and where they can freely join different groups or coalitions without one or the other of the political organizations using exceptional and monopolistic means of unilaterally manipulating the election of representatives can one expect to see genuine representation of social groups or population segments.

If such a mechanism and its institutional guarantee do not exist, there can be no question of genuine representation of the people's interests, in short, there can be no question of democracy. And in the absence of democratic conditions, even the most insistent invocation of "scientific facts" can not guarantee a permanent representation of the rapidly changing demands of the people by a political organization. To the contrary, sooner or later the political organization will become alienated from the interests of the people, will assume an increasingly privileged position, and undergo the transformation into a ruling caste that recruits itself by cooptation.

As will be shown further on, the elimination of the basic democratic principles did not take place only within society as a whole but also within the party itself. The result is *not only the dictatorship of a party but of a limited number of individuals, a "clique," over the entire society.* The critical appraisal of this undemocratic dictatorship as formulated by Rosa Luxemburg shortly after the first practical experiences in postrevolutionary Russia seems even more impressive and justified today than immediately after the October Revolution, since at the time such criticism could be dismissed as being exaggerated and based on insufficient information. Rosa Luxemburg wrote:

> But with the repression of political life in the land as a whole, life in the soviets must also become more and more crippled. Without general elections, without unrestricted freedom of press and assembly, without a free struggle of opinion, life dies out in every public institution, becomes a mere semblance of life, in which only the bureaucracy remains as the active element. Public life gradually falls asleep, a few dozen party leaders of inexhaustible energy and boundless experience direct and rule. Among them, in reality only a dozen outstanding heads do the leading, and an elite of the working class is invited from time to time to meetings where they are to applaud the speeches of the leaders, and to approve proposed resolutions unanimously—at bottom, then, a clique affair—a dictatorship, to be sure, not the dictatorship of the proletariat, however, but only the dictatorship of a handful of politicians, that is a dictatorship in the bourgeois sense, in the sense of the rule of the Jacobins.[34]

She also stressed that "freedom only for the supporters of the government, only for the members of one party—however numerous they may be—is no freedom at all. Freedom is always and exclusively freedom for the one who thinks differently."[35]

STALIN'S SEIZURE OF POWER

Under Stalin's rule the bureaucratic, undemocratic, and repressive characteristics of the Soviet system became increasingly accentuated. However, it would be wrong to conclude that these negative traits are the result of Stalin's despotism. On the contrary, Stalin, whose dangerous personality Lenin himself had warningly referred to in a letter to the Party Congress,[36] had only been able to accede to power and to abuse his power because of the already existing undemocratic situation. Although after Lenin's death several other communist leaders—such as Trotsky, Bukharin, Zinoviev, Kamenev—were quite popular within as well as outside the party, it was Stalin who succeeded in seizing political power and who in the course of time managed to liquidate the other leading party officials whenever they threatened his position. This was only possible because Stalin as General Secretary of the Party[37] came to control the entire party machine and later also the state organs. With all key positions filled by a monopolistic party apparatus that also had the power of dismissing officials, a dependency on this apparatus was to develop that is not conceivable under democratic conditions. Whoever controls this party machine automatically becomes the most powerful individual of the entire political system.[38]

Party leaders such as Trotsky and a few others have recognized this fact only too late. Trotsky, who had a powerful position as minister of war and enjoyed great popularity, was nevertheless the politically weaker man compared to the party secretary. Trotsky believed he could fight ideological battles with Stalin by giving speeches and winning the majority of the party over to his views. He must have realized too late that even the most convincing argument gives in to political pressure exercised—within and without the party—by a person on whose decision the careers of the majority of the party bureaucrats as well as of the leading state officials depended.[39]

Under Stalin's leadership, the bureaucratization of state and party reached inconceivable dimensions. Any true exchange or confrontation of political views gradually died down until the centralization or monopolization of power was complete and absolute. Stalin's personal struggle for power within the party and state hierarchies, his eventually impregnable power position, as well as the increasingly obvious identification of his personal interests with those of socialism all had a decisive influence on the further development of the Soviet Union's political and economic system. Of course, there had been certain preconditions, as mentioned earlier: the backwardness of a country without any democratic traditions and the simplified, insufficiently elaborated theory of socialism. These facts certainly facilitated the establishment of an undemocratic, monopolized, and personalized regime.

From the beginning, Stalin pursued the ambitious goal of strengthening his own position by eliminating all his opponents and rivals. However, in many respects he could hardly hope to measure up to many of the other Bolshevik leaders. He did not possess the theoretical and political capabilities of a Lenin, nor the rhetoric of a Trotsky, nor the ideological knowledge and popularity of a Bukharin. But Stalin's main asset was a kind of scrupulousness tied to a talent for exploiting everybody to his advantage, of playing one person against another until he emerged victorious. Still, he was a typical representative of the party apparatus that enabled him to collect the necessary information on the other leading politicians and to hold the strings of all party activities in his own hand.

Thus, Stalin very soon was the most powerful member of the Zinoviev-Kamenev-Stalin "triumvirate," which had assumed the party leadership at Lenin's request after his first stroke.[40] Stalin astutely introduced a Lenin cult in order to make himself appear still during Lenin's lifetime as his most logical disciple and advocate. Instead of discussing Lenin's theories with him, Stalin made it a point to quote the Master. He selected these quotes so cleverly and so much out of context that they appeared to give his, Stalin's, own political goals a "Leninist" foundation. The formal establishment of a sacrosanct "Marxist-Leninist" doctrine, the pseudoscholastic confrontation of current ideas and theories with these axiomatic "dogmas," the denouncing of differing theories as "anti-Marxist" or "anti-Leninist," and their increasingly cruel political repression all were added by Stalin to the party's existing character traits. He always posed as the guardian of unity and purity of "Lenin's party" while in his function as General Secretary of the Party he skillfully used the resolution of the Tenth Party Congress outlawing "any sort of fractionalism" as a most effective weapon against all his adversaries.

Consistently defending the party apparatus against any attack and criticism, Stalin managed to secure the party's full support for his own position. Shortly before Lenin's death, he skillfully defended the party hierarchy against Trotsky's[41] antibureaucratic criticism, thus endearing himself to the party as its most trustworthy future representative. While Trotsky strove to win the favor of the young and the nonparty circles, Stalin banked on the bureaucratized officials and all those anxious not to lose their powerful positions within the party apparatus. This of course guaranteed him the decisive support of the party.

Throughout his lifetime, Stalin methodically followed this same pattern. His contemporaries who knew him personally and who have described his character in their writings (Lenin, Trotsky, Khrushchev) repeatedly mentioned his lack of principles and his ruthless striving for power. He was not primarily concerned about the interests of the working population and not about the long-term application of political and ideological principles that would have genuinely corresponded to those interests. Very probably Stalin was convinced that his personal power would be the most dependable condition for a "socialist transition" to which all other "principles" had to be subordinated. In order to attain this goal, Stalin did not hesitate to switch from one set of political principles to the exact opposite while making use of certain ideas and theories advocated by other party leaders who just a few years previously had been violently attacked by Stalin himself. However, he was always consistent in one aspect: when setting immediate political goals, Stalin was careful to choose those he knew would get him the full support of the party bureaucracy. The party apparatus, in turn, would then provide him with the necessary majority in all the important power organs as well as for the campaigns Stalin waged against his enemies.

TROTSKY'S DEFEAT

After Lenin's death, Stalin immediately proceeded to eliminate Trotsky, who was his most dangerous rival. To begin with, he opposed Trotsky's theory of "permanent revolution" on the grounds that it was incompatible with the "Leninist" doctrine of the "possible victory of socialism within one country," although Trotsky, of course, never suggested giving up communist rule in Russia but using it to promote socialist revolution in Europe. For without revolutionary expansion, Trotsky[42] believed, communist power was endangered even in Russia itself. The socialist revolution would have to spread especially to the industrially advanced countries in Europe in order to secure the economic assistance without which, according to Trotsky, there could be no socialist development in an economically and socially backward, petty-bourgeois country such as Russia.

I do not want to dwell here on the chances of such spreading of the revolution in Europe but only to underline Trotsky's basic theory and conviction that socialism cannot be built by a handful of professional revolutionaries against the resistance of an absolute majority of the population and without prior significant industrial

development. Besides, Trotsky too had very dogmatic and centralis-
tic views of a socialist system and of nationalized production
planned and controlled by a central planning organ and excluding an
open market. But he believed that this form of socialism could be
possible only in the industrially advanced countries; only these
countries would be able to provide the necessary economic assistance without which industrial and agrarian-technical progress
would seem illusionary in totally impoverished Russia.[43]

Lenin basically shared this view. He, too, waited for an extension of the socialist revolution above all to Germany. Lenin even
considered the New Economic Policy (NEP) introduced by himself as
nothing more but a strategic retreat to an open market system that
would help promote a nonsocialist economy in a Russia of peasant
smallholders until such a time when with the help of economically
advanced *socialist* countries, modern industries and agriculture
could be established in his country. As for the intermediate period,
Lenin even feared that an increase of capitalist accumulation and
production in the Soviet Union might be inevitable.[44]

Trotsky on the other hand did not believe that Russia should
just wait for economic assistance from abroad but should force the
industrialization of the country with the help of its own resources.
This would of course entail considerable difficulties. If the means of
accumulation were to come from agricultural production,[45] according
to Trotsky, this would inevitably lead to peasant resistance and
therefore threaten the dictatorship of the proletariat. For the safeguard of proletarian power in Russia, it seemed therefore imperative
to pursue the development of the socialist world revolution simultaneously with Russia's planned industrialization.

Stalin demagogically interpreted these arguments put forward
by Trotsky in such a way as if Trotsky had said that the safeguard of
the regime depended on revolutionary developments outside of
Russia, as if Trotsky did not believe in the revolutionary potential of
the Russian peasant and the strength and capability of the Russian
proletariat, as if Trotsky opposed Lenin's theory of socialist revolution, and as if his theory were a non-Bolshevik offshoot of Menshev-
ism.[46] Instead of deepening the conflict between proletariat and poor
peasantry that Trotsky supposedly considered to be inevitable, it
was more important to apply Lenin's theory of a "union of the
proletariat with the working peasant masses." In line with the NEP,
the peasants were to be won over to communism by the extension of
the open market and by better supplies of industrial goods. For two
reasons the fight against Trotsky's theory of permanent revolution
was entirely in the interest of the party hierarchy: with Trotsky's
political defeat, a dangerous critic of the party apparatus was

removed, and Stalin's policy of building an independent socialist state reinforced the leading role of the party and of the party machine.[47] With the support of the party and in his role as "consistent" defender of Lenin's NEP policy (while keeping Lenin's last letter, the so-called "Testament," hidden from the party), Stalin managed to strengthen his own position and to obtain Trotsky's political removal at the Thirteenth Party Congress in 1924.

It has to be stressed here, however, that not even Trotsky himself had been able to uncover the real reason for Stalin's powerful position. Although he clearly recognized as the immediate cause Stalin's efficient control and exploitation of the party apparatus, he failed to understand how a party machine can provide its leader with such extensive power, and under what conditions such a situation becomes possible, or would be impossible. To point to the necessity of limiting the power of the apparatus and of strengthening the role of elected bodies must remain wishful thinking, for political reality proves that a political party cannot exist without a bureaucratic apparatus. The preparation of proposals, of party literature, and of organizational charts will always involve extensive and time-consuming work that cannot possibly be supplied by simple workers in addition to their normal working hours. This kind of activity demands the existence of a party apparatus. It is no more than wishful thinking to advocate a "system of Soviets" without planning to establish institutional mechanisms and guaranties against a possible concentration of power within the apparatus.

Also, Trotsky never asked the question whether a people can really be politically alive and develop the necessary initiative as long as all political power is concentrated in one political party. He was no more a democrat than the other communist leaders, and occasionally he even defined the nature of proletarian dictatorship as a hegemony of the working class over the peasant class.[48]. More clearly than all the others, Trotsky demanded that the peasants should be excluded from any political activity and from having their own representatives. Socialism should result from the victory of a minority over the majority of the working class.

This means that the proletarian will is decisive even if it has to be forced on the majority of the people. The danger therefore exists that such a dictatorship is proclaimed without any safeguard against the eventuality that the will of a class may become the will of a clique.

Finally, Trotsky's theory of industrialization also neglects some of man's fundamental economic interests. The first very precise and detailed theory of planned economy was formulated by E. A. Preobrazhensky,[49] one of the most capable among the Trotskyite theoreticians and economists. Rejected by Stalin as Trotskyite deviation, the basic tenets of this theory were nevertheless but unavowedly applied in the later stages of industrialization. The main points that will be dealt with later in more detail are the following: the process of accumulation in the industrial development at the expense of the peasantry; controlled pricing to the disadvantage of agriculture and defined as additional taxation; the concept of socialist methodology as opposed to the theory of value; industrialization in view of a rapid growth of heavy industry and military strength; the elimination of an open market within the industrial sector but systematic control of production relationships with the agricultural sector, and so forth.

Preobrazhensky's theories largely ignore human economic initiative and interest. Rather, the economy resembles a military organization where an efficient planning center controls every move with the help of planning directives and with finance and price regulations without having to worry about adverse reactions from the working population. This obviously implies the assumption that people can be made to behave in any way the state needs them to behave. Preobrazhensky excluded the principle of equivalence (theory of value) with the comment that this principle was already weakened in monopoly capitalism,[50] a rather superficial conclusion as it can only result from ignorance of the actual market functions in late capitalism. However, Preobrazhensky thus provided the theoretical basis for the later arbitrary administration of a planned economy in which a market has no function.

In his political struggle against the Trotskyite opposition, Stalin initially made use of the market theory developed by Bukharin in which he explains the necessity of an exchange of industrial goods for agricultural products on the basis of the theory of value. Thus, Bukharin like Zinoviev supported Stalin in fighting Trotsky's concept of accelerated industrialization. Bukharin especially opposed the Trotskyite theory of "original socialist accumulation" (formulated by Preobrazhensky), a fact Stalin shrewdly exploited at the time. A few years later, Bukharin was eliminated by Stalin with the help of arguments that essentially originated in the Trotskyite theory of industrialization.

THE REMOVAL OF ZINOVIEV AND KAMENEV

Two other leading personalities had to be defeated who in the past repeatedly had opposed the growing power of the party apparatus—Zinoviev and Kamenev. Stalin launched an ideological campaign against these two men before the Fourteenth Congress of the Communist Party in 1925. They had dared to express doubts about the possibility of establishing a socialist economy without foreign assistance, and this at a time when Stalin tried to speed up the development of heavy industry.

Although the previous development had left the government without sufficient means of accumulation of capital—due especially to insufficient productivity increase and bureaucratic mismanagement—Stalin decided on rapid industrialization. He justified this decision with the alleged threat of military intervention by the capitalist states. The fact that an accelerated buildup of heavy industry and of military strength can only be achieved with the help of substantial surplus value and at the expense of a further impoverishment of the population did not deter Stalin from going ahead with his plans. Also, he did not worry about the automatic implication of a further bureaucratization and extension of the administrative machinery—on the contrary, it would ensure him the bureaucrats' loyal support.

As soon as Kamenev and Zinoviev had expressed their doubts about Stalin's decision, they were denounced as "enemies of socialist progress," although shortly before Zinoviev had supported Stalin against the Trotskyite policy of industrialization. At that time Stalin had opposed those tendencies because he sought to eliminate Trotsky from the political scene. He had argued that Lenin would have tended to promote agriculture rather than industry. Only two years later and regardless of the fact that economic conditions had hardly changed, Stalin launched his campaign for industrialization. Did Zinoviev remind him of his own refusal to believe that it would be possible to establish a socialist industry without foreign help? Anyhow, he certainly knew how to turn this theory against Zinoviev by using very scholastic argumentation. He made Zinoviev's opinion appear to be the expression of lacking confidence in the strength of the Soviet people. It was important to distinguish between the "possibility of establishing a socialist society in one country" and the "final victory of socialism in one country".[51] Although the Soviet Union was capable of building a strong industry through its own efforts, socialism would not be *definitely* secured unless socialist revolution had triumphed in a few other countries as well.

At the Fourteenth Party Congress in 1925, the Zinoviev faction confronted Stalin and demanded a slowdown in the process of industrialization combined with the liquidation of capitalist elements, especially the rich peasantry, the *kulaks*. Sokolnikov's[52] oppositional plan proposed to give priority to the food industry as a rapid means of accumulating capital that could later be used as a basis for increased industrial production. If at the same time taxation of capitalist elements had been raised, socialist industrialization could have proceeded without the incredible impoverishment of the working population in later years, and without the past—and present—exploitation of the Soviet Union's natural resources.

At this point it becomes already very clear that the bureaucratic apparatus had been conceived to serve the hasty establishment of a military power basis while cynically ignoring human needs and the living conditions of the population. The stagnation typical of communism in other countries that we see today led Stalin and the entire bureaucratic machinery to concentrate exclusively on their own political interests while blatantly underestimating the factor of the "working population" within as well as outside the country. The basic theory of Marxism that socialism can only develop on the basis of conscious support from the majority of the working people and their basic interests will always remain foreign to the bureaucratic apparatus. The idea that socialism in its actual application should be attractive above all to the working masses at home and abroad will always be replaced by the bureaucrats with the simplified concept that the state must defend socialism against internal as well as external threats by means of police surveillance and military force. Typically, a bureaucrat will not reason that *actual* changes in the living conditions of the working individual in a socialist state would be the most impressive feature in the eyes of the working class in capitalist countries whatever the basic conditions for a successful military defense of the socialist state. On the contrary, the bureaucrat is inclined to view the progress of socialism in the world—just as in his own country—mainly as a result of strengthening and consolidating the power apparatus and the military establishment.

Therefore, from the very start Stalin's main concern was not economic improvements for the working classes but his own political interests and those of his bureaucratized party apparatus. Stalin's personal struggle for power as well as the ruthless exercise of authority by the bureaucracy explains the consistent refusal of all proposals submitted by Stalin's opponents. Logically, Stalin's opponents automatically were adversaries of the majority of party officials and had to be declared enemies of "socialism."

For this reason Zinoviev and Kamenev and their followers were not simply regarded as proponents of an economic plan that had been rejected but they had to be unmasked and eliminated (*razgromit*) as "enemies of the party" and "advocates of capitalism."[53] As far as Stalin was concerned, there was no alternative.

Thus Stalin, with carefully planned political moves, gradually strengthened his personal rule. Methodically extending the hierarchies of both party and state while at the same time eliminating the oposition, he systematically worked toward the consolidation of an autocratic and monopolistic state. The basis of this dictatorship was Stalin's ruthlessly enforced industrialization of the country, the resulting increase in productivity[54] being absorbed primarily by a buildup of military strength.

In pursuing his goal Stalin did not worry about the human factor. The economic situation of the working masses—peasants as well as workers—deteriorated instead of improving, voluntary support for socialist progress was replaced by increasing opposition, and the idea of socialism lost its appeal to the workers in other countries. Stalin had long been convinced that socialism, which he himself could conceive of only in the form of *state monopolism*, could be enforced, nationally and internationally, *only by means of political and administrative power.*

Without letting up in his fight against the Trotskyites, Stalin began de facto to apply their theory of industrialization. Increasing needs for investment, the rapidly growing capital goods industry and the slowdown in consumer goods production were made possible by cutting down on consumption, by decreasing supplies of consumer goods to the countryside, and by reducing the amount of consumer goods that made up part of the workers' wages, meaning a cut in their real wages. Preobrazhensky had theoretically prepared this policy by stating his conviction that in the long run it would serve "socialism."[55] Although Stalin liquidated the Trotskyites as "class enemies," he nevertheless made reckless use of their theories without ever giving them credit for this in his political and ideological argumentations.

The country's accelerated industrialization resulted in galloping inflation. Though prices of industrial products were kept down by the government (they were lowered in 1923), agricultural prices increased steadily. Despite the price increase, the middle income peasants in 1927 still had a lower average income than the urban worker.[56] Receiving fewer and fewer industrial goods in exchange for their inflationary money, the peasants rapidly lost interest in increasing their production. In order to stop prices from rising, the Soviet leadership decided in 1927-28 to lower the purchase price for grain. Simultaneously, the government applied economic pressure by raising taxes, which led to widespread selling strikes by the peasants. Stalin hoped to break their resistance by administrative measures.

RETREAT FROM NEP

The administrative measures signaled the transition from the New Economic Policy, the open-market relationship between town and countryside, to administratively enforced requisitions of the peasants' produce. Although classified as "emergency measures," the new coercive methods in reality amounted to a permanent system of planned production orders and delivery obligations. The excessively high quotas undermined the open market in agricultural products. As soon as the peasants tried to sell part of their production at higher prices in the market, their delivery quotas were raised, with the result that the peasants' incentive to produce and to market more food rapidly disappeared.

The enforced quotas lowered consumption not only in rural areas but also in the cities, where food rationing cards had to be issued. While overall consumption was thus substantially reduced, the government increased its export of Soviet grain in order to obtain foreign exchange for financing its policy of accelerated industrialization.

But the controversial system of state-planned agricultural production and forced food deliveries that corresponded perfectly to the interests and working methods of the bureaucratic apparatus could hardly be based on the disrupted private property of millions of smallholder peasants. Since this form of production planning and distribution was considered "socialist"—whereas free-market relations were only acceptable as a necessary compromise with private property owners—Stalin had to go one step further. The transition to "socialist" planning of production and delivery in the agricultural sector, which had been set in motion by accelerated industrialization and by reduced government grain purchases, now had to be provided with a "socialist" ownership basis. The signal was set for immediate forced collectivization. While in earlier years there had been constant talk of voluntary transition to cooperative production on the basis of gradual mechanization of agriculture, now all of a sudden the small peasant was declared mature enough and willing to make the change to collective agriculture—even without mechanization. Allegedly it was only the rich capitalist peasant, the *kulak*, who opposed the development of a collective farming system. Therefore, collectivization had to go hand in hand with the liquidation of the rich peasant as a class (*rozkulatschenie*). In reality, these measures were intended to make the collectives *kolkhozes* more attractive to the small and middle income peasants: Instead of the agricultural machinery and the tractors [57] promised by the state, they received the cattle, the farming tools, and the land of the *kulaks*.

The results of this "socialization" were mass slaughterings of livestock,[58] the burning and destruction of farms, desperate revolts by the peasants, and ruthless and bloody suppression by the government. The best among the farmers, also from the ranks of the middle income peasants, were destroyed not only economically but physically, or deported to Siberia. Collectivization was carried out within no time by means of brutal threats and repression.[59] During 1930, 55 percent of all farms were collectivized, and by 1934 the figure had reached as much as 93 percent. Not only the kulaks but also the small and middle income peasants were liquidated as a class of independent producers although they had never exploited anybody.

The kolkhozes were required to fulfill enormous delivery quotas at such low prices that the system amounted to a state-controlled exploitation of the peasants. Stalin openly admitted that the artificially created differential between the high prices for industrial products sold to the peasants and the low state-controlled prices for agricultural products purchased from the peasants was an additional, indirect taxation of the peasants designed to finance the country's industrialization.[60] For many years, the state purchase prices for the incredibly high, state-enforced deliveries of agricultural products by the kolkhozes were so low, according to Khrushchev, that they were not even sufficient to cover the peasants' original costs.[61] One result among others was an unimaginable impoverishment of the peasants leading to famines, resistance, and revolts. But all these acts of despair on the part of the peasant population were brutally repressed.

The government forced the peasants to belong to a kolkhoze and those who tried to escape were severly punished. In fact, a system of identity cards and travel restrictions throughout the country substantially limited people's most basic right to free movement. In practice this policy meant a return to forced labor, which Lenin himself had rejected.

Stalin never admitted to the obvious deviation from Lenin's NEP and especially from the concept of the sacred alliance between the working class and the peasant masses, nor to the transition to a policy of exploitation and suppression of the peasants by the state. On the contrary, Stalin continued to pretend that this alliance served as the social foundation for the dictatorship of the proletariat. When Bukharin criticized the administrative measures enforced against the peasants and their exploitation for the sake of the country's industrialization, Stalin used these arguments to get rid of this last of his most powerful political rivals.

As late as December 1927, though, at the Fifteenth Party Congress, Bukharin had supported Stalin in fighting the so-called

Trotsky-Zinoviev opposition, and he had even voted for their expulsion from the party.[62] He had never approved of Trotsky's theory of industrialization at the expense of the peasants. When after the Fifteenth Party Congress Bukharin published a number of articles rejecting Trotsky's agricultural policy, he indirectly attacked Stalin's policy as "military-feudal exploitation of the peasants." This, he argued, would necessarily break up the alliance between the proletariat and the peasants.[63]

Bukharin especially warned against giving up the basic principles of NEP and against an excessively accelerated industrialization that would upset the market balance between industry and agriculture. In his article "Notes of an economist," Bukharin stressed the fact that the highest and most permanent growth rate could be obtained by coordinating industrial and agricultural development[64] in such a way that the increase in production in one area becomes the basis for an increase in production in the other area, and vice versa. This would lead to the gradual establishment of agricultural cooperatives on the modern technical basis of collective mass production.

Bukharin's theory was based on the assumption that socialist production cannot be introduced by administrative measures, noneconomical pressure, or repression, but will automatically prove superior to private production methods in view of its economic and social advantages. The peasants would be easily convinced of these economic and social advantages of collective production by use of a competitive market and by the attraction of modern agricultural machinery and techniques produced and developed by a modernized socialist industry. As early as 1925, Bukharin had quoted von Mises: "If the communists want to control production with orders, with a stick, their policy will fail, and it already shows signs of failure."[65]

However, at the same time Bukharin rejected Mises' theory that the development of a market would lead back to capitalism. He believed that the working class cannot be won over to socialism against its will but only by stimulating its own interest in improving working and living conditions by means of higher collective productivity, collective old-age care, etc. Therefore, he demanded simultaneously with the development of NEP a change in the socialist state's politics and especially a stop to its repressive and dictatorial activities.[66]

Bukharin's political platform, his criticism of the state's repressive measures and policy of coercion, and of the incredible bureaucratization and growing concentration of power in the party apparatus became increasingly threatening and intolerable to Stalin. He could not accept the theory of gradual elimination of private production by competition with socialist production, nor could he approve of the development of light industry in coordination with agricultural production as a starting point and source of accumulation for building up heavy industries,[67] and he certainly could not tolerate the idea of the state's gradual democratization and liberalization.

Not only did Stalin think in dogmatic terms of completely simplified "friend-enemy" categories—an "enemy" being defined as not agreeing with Stalin's concept of "socialism"—but his actions were essentially dictated by personal power considerations that led him to ruthlessly liquidate any of his critics. Such thinking and such interests could only result in a *theory of intensified class struggle* within as well as outside the country. Logically, Bukharin and his followers had to be put on trial as advocates of "class peace with the capitalists."[68] In November 1929, Bukharin was expelled from the Politburo. Stalin had rid himself of his last major antagonist and rival.

POLITICS OF INTENSIFIED CLASS STRUGGLE

Bukharin's theories were certainly right concerning the usefulness of open-market relations between industry and agriculture, between city and countryside, as a basis for promoting the economic and social advantages of socialist production. But his ideas were unrealistic under the given political and ideological circumstances. Bukharin's theoretical assumptions at that time were necessarily still rather biased and full of compromises; they did not touch on the deeply rooted concepts of state ownership in industry and its centrally planned control, and even less on the conception of dictatorship of the proletariat by means of the monopolized power of the Communist Party. Of course, this should not be interpreted as criticism of Bukharin for he was tried as a "capitalist traitor" just on the basis of his theories. But these theoretical half-truths help explain the apparent weakness of Bukharin's position against Stalin's argumentation.

Industrial production controlled by an immense centralized and bureaucratized apparatus, without any market incentives, understandably could not evolve in a way that would have been favorable to a gradual elimination of private production. The resulting inefficiency and declining productivity hardly ensured the needed capital development, and the slow industrial growth could not provide enough stimulation for agricultural production. However, without market competition and the stimulation of independent industrial enterprises, it was impossible to ensure structurally flexible supplies of industrial products, especially of modern agricultural means of production that would have been the necessary incentive for the peasants to voluntarily make the transition to technically attractive collective mass production. In the absence of all these conditions, the agricultural sector like all the others would only undergo a normal socioeconomic differentiation, with the rich peasants getting richer and the poor peasants getting poorer.

In all probability, Bukharin himself and other theoreticians would have reached the obvious conclusions and would have recognized the usefulness of a market even within the industrial sector or, in other words, of a necessary degree of independence of industrial collective market enterprises. However, by its very nature such a development was threatening to the bureaucratic apparatus, for it has been, is, and will always be essentially antibureaucratic. The precondition for such a development is an increasing democratization in the economic as well as political sectors. Therefore, Bukharin's first criticism of the bureaucratic apparatus earned him Stalin's and the party's everlasting enmity.[69]

While still working at his theory and criticism, Bukharin was not yet fully aware of the antisocial and terrorist consequences of bureaucratism, nor of the fact that Stalin's policy very accurately reflected the logic of the bureaucratic system. He was not conscious of the mechanism that in a one-party system the so-called dictatorship of the proletariat necessarily degenerates into a dictatorship of the party machine and of its personified ruler whose sole reliable societal support was the bureaucratic power apparatus.

When the completely bureaucratized industry was not capable of successfully competing with and replacing capitalist production, and since the state could not purchase sufficient grain through the mechanism of a free market, the typically bureaucratic approach to coping with the situation was to eliminate production relations and to liquidate the rich peasantry. When the state government was unable to provide sufficient machinery or new techniques for modern collective production, and since the forced state delivery of foodstuffs by millions of individual small-scale producers could not be organized and controlled efficiently, the rapid and forced collectivization of the peasants seemed an equally "normal" reaction of the bureaucracy. And when all these measures encountered the desperate opposition of the peasants and the hungry masses, the bureaucratic reaction understandably was a continuous extension and strengthening of the power apparatus justified with the *theory of the intensification of the class struggle even after the total liquidation of the bourgeoisie.*

It goes without saying that anybody had to be declared a "class enemy" and liquidated who under such circumstances was trying to oppose the uneconomical and antisocial policy of the government, or to defend the interests of the working population, or to suggest a substantially different approach to industrialization while criticizing the bureaucratic methods. Thus, Bukharin inevitably was denounced as a "representative of petty bourgeois interests and protector of the *kulaks*" and put on trial for his alleged opposition to socialist collectivization. Stalin, who once had criticized Trotsky for considering the small peasantry as a petty-bourgeois antisocialist class and for wanting to subject this class to the dictate of the proletarian state rather than to win it over—Stalin now adopted exactly the same position. With incredible demagogy he liquidated Bukharin, who from the very beginning had consistently fought this theory and its later application. Having blamed Trotsky in the past for underestimating "the revolutionary socialist potential of the small peasantry," Stalin now accused Bukharin of not recognizing "the capitalist tendencies of the peasantry."[70]

Bukharin's criticism was the last openly expressed criticism of Stalin voiced by a member of the highest leadership group. After his political defeat, the so-called unity of the party was achieved, which in reality meant Stalin's personal power. From now on Stalin ruled as an autocrat. In the—officially—highest party organs he was surrounded by stooges, and even the slightest critical remark was viewed as the expression of enemy subversion.[71]

Several show trials like the one of the "saboteurs of Shakhty" in the coal mining district of the Donets Basin were staged to prove the alleged class enemy's hostile and harmful activities and thus to provide justified reasons for a further intensification of the class struggle. The unmasking of enemies and their acts of sabotage was designed to distract the growing discontent of the population from the real causes of the largely insufficient supplies and the low standard of living while directing people's resentment to the "people's enemies" uncovered by Stalin.[72]

At the Seventeenth Party Congress in 1934, Bukharin, Rykov, Tomsky, Zinoviev, and Kamenev had to implicate themselves by self-accusations in a most degrading way. It was their ultimate attempt not only to remain in the party but above all to be able to fight Stalin from within the organization. Stalin, who feared these intelligent and experienced politicians and wanted to keep them from exercising any further political influence, reacted to this incident with a most devilish attack, setting off a hardly imaginable wave of mass terror throughout the country. In December 1934, Stalin instigated the assassination of Kirov, who had been totally loyal to him but who constituted a threat for Stalin because of his growing popularity with the people. Kirov's murder was then conveniently explained by an alleged conspiracy involving Trotsky, Kamenev, Zinoviev, and others, and served as a pretext for the first of a series of perfectly orchestrated show trials.[73] The confessions extracted by means of torture, blackmail, and fabricated "evidence" were then presented in a vast propaganda campaign intended to make the population believe in an extensive and foreign-influenced, anti-soviet conspiracy.[74] This approved method was to be applied later by other communist countries, becoming one of the system's essential characteristics.

Stalin thus triggered a wave of terror throughout the country to which hundreds of thousands of innocent people fell victim.[75] Since that time, the persecutions have never stopped completely, and denunciations, arbitrary measures by the security organs, and spying became a depressing feature of daily life. Stalin has established a system characterized by terror and fear, making the term "communism" synonymous with "inhumanity," "brutality," and "injustice."

However, Stalin could never have achieved such a position of power and he could never have exercised his power with such brutality if he had not been able to interpret and to satisfy the interests of the party apparatus under the most differing circumstances. Sudden shifts, skillful retreats frim certain political goals that earlier had been advocated as principles of party politics, adoption of political lines that in earlier years he had fought as being anti-Leninist, alliances with certain politicians against other politicians just to turn around shortly thereafter and liquidate the former allies by using the arguments of those he had been fighting before helped extend Stalin's power only because they served the interests of the party apparatus as well.

The consistent defense of the principles of the New Economic Policy even after Lenin's death against Trotsky's theories of industrialization on the basis of peasant exploitation was entirely in the interest of the party machine. As long as the party apparatus was relatively small and weak and could not have existed without the voluntary support of large classes of society, industrialization against the resistance of the peasantry would not have been in its interest. For the same reason, Trotsky's proposal of rapid industrialization on the basis of centralized capital accumulation derived from agriculture had no chance of being accepted.

On the other hand, it was one of the priorities of the party apparatus to fight any attempt at decentralization and independence of industrial enterprises by means of workers' councils and to promote the systematic establishment of a highly centralized control organization in the industrial sector. Of all the Bolshevik leaders,

Stalin was the most skillful and consistent in understanding and defending these contradictory interests of the party bureaucracy.

When the bureaucracy became aware of the fact that it would be impossible to further extend the socialist world revolution and that it was in danger of losing any prospect for its own future existence, Stalin, against Trotsky's doctrine of permanent revolution, assured the bureaucracy of its future by setting the goal of "achieving socialism in one country." Again, he proved the better analyst of the bureaucracy's psychological makeup.

The greatest threats to the bureaucratic apparatus occurred when in the late 1920s the peasant resistance endangered the food supply to the cities, and when Bukharin demanded an extended market mechanism as well as a debureaucratization of the industry in view of more flexible and economically efficient production processes. Again Stalin did not hesitate to save the apparatus, and he even extended its range of power by rejecting all NEP principles and ordering the transition to forced collectivization. This unexpected and unprepared process of collectivization helped create the right conditions for state administration and control of agricultural production, for police requisitions of agricultural products, for an unprecedented exploitation of the peasants, for a more speedy financing of the country's industrialization, as well as for an extension of the bureaucratic administration and repression apparatus. Trotsky's theory of industrialization though earlier rejected by Stalin and by Bukharin became reality once the apparatus had grown powerful enough to repress any resistance. The suppression, in turn, was a condition for increased power of the apparatus itself. Trotsky at that time had already been politically liquidated; now Bukharin represented the greatest threat to bureaucracy and he had to be eliminated.

Created and protected by Stalin, the party apparatus unfailingly backed him in all critical situations, elevated him to supreme power, and idolized and glorified him. The party created the personality cult surrounding Stalin and subsequently used it to liquidate all opponents to bureaucratic centralism.

But even the elimination of the Stalin cult after the dictator's death was in the interest of the party apparatus. The fact that the population might identify the concept of socialism with Stalin's personality was a potential threat to the system. There was the dangerous possibility that after the death of the "leader" the population may have been less ready to starve for "socialism" and to accept without criticism all the economic shortcomings of the regime. In addition, all those who had been persecuted by Stalin and had survived the purges, and the relatives and friends of his countless victims were a potential threat to the system that was now left without Stalin's protection. Consequently, the new representative of the apparatus had no choice but to destroy Stalin's image in order to put the party and its system above all criticism.

When Khrushchev criticized the Stalin cult, endeavoring to separate Stalin's personality and actions from the "idea of socialism" and condemning Stalin's crimes, he took the wind out of the critics' sail. Khrushchev represented those party circles that could not directly be implicated in Stalin's criminal activities and thus could afford to publicly condemn Stalin. He became the apparent defender of all Stalinist victims but above all he was the savior of the party bureaucracy. Especially in the party's interest was the rapid liquidation of Berija, the head of the state security organs. His succession to Stalin would have endangered numerous party officials, threatened the supremacy of the party apparatus, and possibly resulted in the predominance of the organs of state security within the entire power system.

By criticizing the personality cult, the existing latent dissatisfaction of the population was channeled away from its actual cause, the bureaucratic system, toward a secondary factor, Stalin's personality. As we shall see later on, all the essential economic and political traits of the bureaucratic system have been maintained to this very day. Despite the unmasking and condemnation of criminal and terrorist Stalinism at the Twentieth Party Congress of the Soviet Communist Party, only the *forms* of repression have changed slightly. The essential principles as established by Lenin and extended under Stalin that made Stalinist terror possible in the first place have not only not been criticized by Khrushchev, on the contrary, they have been defended by him.[76]

The purpose of the following analysis of the general characteristics of the communist system is to prove that these traits have not been removed following the criticism of Stalin's rule, that they have existed in their beginnings before Stalin even seized power, and that consequently they are the result of a simplified and faulty doctrine which subsequently has been perverted in its application.

NOTES

1. V. I. Lenin, "On Left-Wing Childishness and Petty-Bourgeois Mentality," *Collected Works.*

2. Lenin, "Draft of the Party Program of the Russian Communist Party," *Coll. Works* (March 1918).

3. Russel in *Leninuv odkaz* [Lenin's testament], p. 172.

4. As Lenin's underestimation and simplification of the entire problem of democracy becomes more evident today, the dangerous aspect of his habit to dismiss his socialist opponents on this issue as class enemies or similar (razgromit) stands out more than ever before. Compare Lenin's polemic against Kautsky.

5. W. Harich, Zur Kritik der revolutionaeren Ungeduld [On the critique of revolutionary impatience] (Basel, 1971), p. 13.

6. Lenin, "Draft of the Party Program of the Russian Communist Party."

7. Lenin, "Extraordinary Seventh Party Congress of the CPR," Coll. Works.

8. Lenin, "Second All-Russian Miners' Conference," Coll. Works.

9. Lenin, "Fourth Anniversary of the October Revolution," Coll. Works.

10. Lenin, "Seventh Moscow City Party Conference," Coll. Works.

11. Lenin, "Fourth Anniversary of the October Revolution."

12. Lenin, "The State and Revolution," Coll. Works.

13. Lenin, "Our International and Domestic Political Situation and the Tasks of the Party," Coll. Works; ibid., "Better less, but better."

14. Lenin, "Speech at the Third All Russian Conference of Economists," Coll. Works.

15. A. Jugow, Die Volkswirtschaft der Sowjetunion und ihre Probleme [The economy of the Soviet Union and its problems] (Dresden, 1929), p. 70.

16. Article of Dzerzinsky in Pravda, Jan. 1, 1926, as quoted in Jugow, ibid., p. 69.

17. Lenin, "Ninth Party Congress of the CPR," Coll. Works.

18. Lenin, "Extraordinary Seventh Party Congress of the CPR."

19. Lenin, "Second All-Russian Miners' Conference."

20. See also O. Anweiler, Arbeiterdemokratie oder Parteidiktatur [worker democracy or party dictatorship], eds. F. Kool and E. Oberlaender (Munich, 1972), 1:61-68.

21. Schlapnikow, "Die Organisation der Volkswirtschaft und die Aufgaben der Gewerkschaften" [Organization of the economy and tasks of the trade unions], ibid., p. 165.

22. Lenin, "Speech at the Third All-Russian Shipping Workers' Conference," Coll. Works.

23. Lenin, "The Next Tasks of the Soviet Regime," Coll. Works.

24. Lenin, "The Crisis of the Party," Coll. Works; A. Kollontai, "Ueber Buerokratismus und die Eigeninitiative der Massen" [On bureaucratism and self-initiative of the masses] in Kool and Oberlaender, Arbeiterdemokratie oder Parteidiktatur, 1:225.

25. Lenin, "The Tax in Kind," Coll. Works.

26. Lenin, "Second All-Russian Miners' Conference."

27. "Theses of the Workers' Opposition at the Tenth Party Congress," in Kool and Oberlaender, Arbeiterdemokratie oder Parteidiktatur, 1:73.

28. Lenin, "Extraordinary Seventh Party Congress of the CPR."

29. To cite an example, the movement and uprising of the workers and sailors in Kronstadt was described in such a simplified manner as early as 1921, during Lenin's lifetime. See also R. Rocker and E. Goldmann, Der Bolschewismus: Verstaatlichung der Revolution [Bolshevism: nationalization of the revolution] (Berlin, 1968), p. 99.

30. Kool and Oberlaender, Arbeiterdemokratie oder Parteidiktatur. 1:69.

31. See also Rocker and Goldmann, Der Bolschewismus, p. 102.

32. Lenin, "Speech at the Railroad and Shipping Workers' Conference," Coll. Works.

33. Lenin, "More on Trade Unions," Coll. Works.

34. Rosa Luxemburg, "The Russian Revolution." In Rosa Luxemburg Speaks, pp. 389-391. New York: Pathfinder Press, 1970.

35. Ibid.

36. Lenin, "Letter to the Party Congress," *Coll. Works.*

37. The First Secretary of the Party Central Committee was originally responsible for the organizational tasks within the party, the control of the party apparatus' activities, the preparation of material for the party's central organs, and therefore for all aspects of cadre politics. To these tasks was added later the cadre policy in all major organs of state government and administration. Thus, Stalin succeeded in concentrating immense powers in his hands, which Lenin already pointed out warningly.

38. L. Trotsky, *Stalin.*

39. See also Alec Nove, *An Economic History of the USSR* (London, 1969).

40. In the Soviet Union as well as in other "socialist" countries, the real ruler emerging from the so-called collective party leadership has always been the man who dominated the party apparatus and, thus, cadre politics. This was true in the case of Khrushchev, Brezhnev, Novotny, Ulbricht, and others.

41. *History of the Communist Party of the Soviet Union* [Bolshevik] (Moscow, 1939).

42. Trotsky, quoted from J. V. Stalin, *Problems of Leninism.*

43. Trotsky, "Theses on Industry, 1923," in *A Documentary History of Communism*, ed. R. V. Daniels (New York, 1960), p. 234.

44. Lenin, "Tenth Party Congress of the CPR" *Coll. Works.*

45. Trotsky, "Theses on Industry."

46. Stalin, "The October Revolution and the Strategy of the Russian Communists," in *Problems of Leninism* (Moscow, 1947).

47. Stalin, "On the Foundations of Leninism," ibid.

48. Trotsky, *Stalin.*

49. See in particular E. A. Preobrazhenski, *Ekonomitscheskije krizisy pri NEPe* (Moscow, 1924); *Novaja ekonomika* (Moscow, 1926); *Problema chozjajstvennogo ravnovesije pri konkretnom kapitalizme i v sovjetskoj sisteme* (Moscow).

50. See E. A. Preobazhenski, *The New Economics* (Oxford, 1965), p. 160.

51. Stalin, *Problems of Leninism.*

52. See Central Committee of the Communist Party of the USSR, *History of the Communist Party of the Soviet Union* [Bolsheviks] (Moscow, 1952).

53. Ibid.

54. Ibid.

55. Preobrazhenski, *The New Economics*, p. 195.

56. See data given by Strumilin and Lifsic, *Planovoje chozjajstvo*, no. 3 (1928); *Vestnik financov*, no. 2 (1929); *Bolshevik*, no. 2-3 (1929).

57. According to the State Archives for Economy in Moscow, two-thirds of the *kolkhozes* did not have one single tractor in 1928.

58. In the first phase of mass collectivization in late 1929, 1.6 million horses had been butchered, and by January 1, 1931, 3 million more. Between 1929 and 1933, the number of cattle was reduced by half, sheep and goats by two-thirds. In 1933, livestock numbered less than in the year of famine, 1922. *Narodnoje Chozjajstov USSR* [The economy of the USSR] (Moscow, 1956), p. 118.

59. N. J. Nemakov, *Kommunistitscheskaja Partija—organisator massovogo kolchosnogo dvischenija* [The Communist Party organization of the kolkhoze mass-movement] (Moscow, 1966), p. 20.

60. Stalin, "On Industrialization and the Grain Problem," speech from July 9, 1928, *Coll. Works*, vol. 11.

61. See also N. S. Khrushchev, in *Izvestia*, March 7, 1964.

62. Excluded from the party were Trotsky, Zinoviev, Radek, Preobrazhensky, Rakovsky, Piatakov, Serebriakov, I. Smirnov, Kamenev, Sarkis, Safasov, Smilga, Sapronov, V. Smirnov, and others.

63. See *Resolutions and Decisions of the Communist Party of the Soviet Union* (Toronto, 1974), 2:34.

64. Bukharin, "Zametki ekonomista" [Notes of an economist], *Pravda*, September 30, 1928.

65. Bukharin, "O novoj ekonomitscheskoj politike i naschich zadatschach" [On the New Economic Policy and our Tasks], *Bolshevik*, no. 8 (1925), p. 8.

66. Bukharin, "Chozjajstvennyj rost i problema rabotschekrestjanskogo bloka" [Economic growth and the problems of the workers and peasants bloc], *Bolshevik* (November 5, 1924), p. 33.

67. See especially the article by L. Schanin, "Ekonomitscheskaja priroda nasego beztovaija" [The economic nature of our commodity shortage], *Ekonomitscheskoje obozrenije* 11 (1924), pp. 25-39.

68. *History of the Communist Party of the Soviet Union*, p. 355.

69. In September 1923, after Lenin's first heart attack, a meeting was held in Kislowodsk by a number of leading politicians opposed to Stalin's and the party apparatus' increasing power. Zinoviev and Bukharin had prepared a list of measures designed to restrict this bureaucratic power. Evidently, their plan remained unsuccessful, and neither the apparatus nor Stalin forgot about this meeting. All the participants were liquidated by Stalin.

70. Stalin, "Questions of the Agrarian Policy in the USSR," in *Problems of Leninism*.

71. See also N. S. Khrushchev, Khruschev's Secret Speech at the Twentieth Party Congress, Moscow, February 25, 1956.

72. Ibid.

73. *History of the Communist Party of the Soviet Union*; Khrushchev's Secret Speech at the Twentieth Party Congress.

74. *History of the Communist Party of the Soviet Union*.

75. N. S. Khrushchev, Khrushchev's Secret Speech at the Twentieth Party Congress.

76. Ibid.

2
CHARACTERISTICS OF
COMMUNIST BUREAUCRACY

PERSONAL POWER INTERESTS OF THE PARTY FUNCTIONARIES

The average Communist Party member, especially in Western countries, as well as many left-wing revolutionary youths, usually react with disbelief when they hear of bureaucratization and of political interests on the part of communist functionaries in the "socialist" states. In most cases, these people have emotional rather than rational ties to the communist movement. They see the communist functionaries as honest people who would not be corrupted by the bourgeois power, or who personally suffered persecution while fighting capitalism. These people cannot, and will not believe that this integrity could have disappeared after the communist takeover. For some time, this attitude was typical also of "old" communists in the "socialist" countries. However, their attitude is no longer based on personal experience because the ordinary party member rarely has any direct personal contact with high party functionaries. Such concepts are mostly formed by propaganda that is capable of shaping the trust and devotion not only of party members but of the broad mass of the people to an extent that it even creates a hero cult of the leader (Stalin, Mao Tse-tung, Castro). The question is certainly justified why this should be only a propagandistic glorification and why those leaders should not be the same consistent defenders of the people's interests even after the revolution. It is mostly argued that the leaders themselves should be interested in defending the people's cause. Also, many people in the West are even ready to accept the possibility of serious errors and shortcomings in "socialism." Although they cannot deny the existence of gigantic bureaucratic machines, they do not blame this fact on the leaders. On the contrary, it is always pointed out that the leaders themselves are criticizing and fighting the system's short-comings.

However, there is confusion already at this point as to the formulation of the problem and the argumentation involved, so that it becomes necessary to clarify the issue. To begin with, the question has to be asked if it is at all possible to arrive at a coordinated, efficient, and successful economic development under the conditions of a highly centralized management of all economic and other social activities. In my book *The Third Way—Marxist-Leninist Theory and Modern Industrial Society*,[1] I have described in detail why an economic system organized along these lines cannot really function well, and why it is less efficient than capitalist economies. Even the most qualified and honest leader cannot remove the essential short-comings and contradictions of this system. The other question is to what extent the leaders are able to recognize the essential contradic-tions of a given system, and to what extent they are willing or allowed to essentially change such a system. Let's leave the question aside as to what motives, personalities, abilities, and so forth the leaders had before they seized power. It is certain that in this respect too many facts have been idealized by the masses themselves, or for their benefit. In every political movement there are reliable and unreliable people, honest fighters and opportunists, people who put the population's interests above their own interests, and others who intend to use the people's interests only as a cover for their personal ambitions. Undoubtedly, the personalities of the leaders have an influence on the movement both before and after the revolution or seizure of power,[2] an influence that will be all the more negative the more egotistical and hungry for power the most influential among the leaders is.

Even though Stalin's personality had an immensely negative influence on the postrevolutionary development of not only the party but also the entire Soviet system, it would be wrong to overestimate this influence. There is a reason for the fact that the present rulers and their ideologists try to make Stalin appear to be responsible for all the adverse manifestations of the past, and that they see the causes of the consequential abuses of his power in the so-called Stalin cult. In reality, however, independently of Stalin's specifically negative traits all leaders of communist systems without exception have something in common that cannot be the result of a chance faulty character.

They all have in common their close relationship with the party and the firm conviction that the party must secure "socialism" or the "dictatorship of the proletariat" by filling all key positions in the new government. The concept that only party members and, among those, only the "professional revolutionaries"—meaning the party apparatus—are apt to decide *who* and *what* benefit socialism and *who* and *what* are harmful to it is based on the conviction that a *communist elite is indispensable.* And this same conviction, which became the basic tenet of communist practice in all communist-ruled countries, is the shadow no high communist functionary has so far been able to escape. For this principle a priori sets limits to an exposure of the mistakes and shortcomings of the system by any particular communist leader.

The communist system cannot function as long as it is tied to a number of specific and *essential principles*, that is, as long as it does not undergo some *essential* change. This essential change, however, does not necessarily mean the transition to a capitalist system; on the contrary, it should create the preconditions for establishing a truly *socialist* system. But to expose the necessity of such an essential change within the system is not part of the leaders' functions who, at the head and with the help of their parties have established the communist systems, or who have later been elevated to fill the system's key posts. As head of the party whose leadership role is one of the essential principles of the system, a leader can no longer bring about a change of the system resulting in the disappearance of the "leading role of the party."[3] This constitutes the basic dilemma faced by all communist leaders in their "attempts" at eliminating the system's shortcomings.

Even if we assume that communist leaders have different personalities, moral profiles, and motives, that some of them really care for the working classes' needs and interests but that others merely use the people's interests as a pretext for furthering their own political ambitions, we have to recognize that these leaders always had, and will have, one trait in common: in their own actions they are dependent on the party, that is, on the "professional revolutionaries," on the party apparatus. Consequently, the leaders could only act in ways not directed against the party apparatus. Had they acted against the interests of the party apparatus, they would no longer have been communist leaders, which would have implied that they would have needed some other social support for achieving certain social goals.

This mechanism as described here is not an artificially created issue but illustrates a permanent dilemma faced by various communist leaders. Time and again attempts have been made to solve this problem but so far without success. It goes without saying that this dilemma did not originate in the Stalin era nor with Novotny, Ulbricht, Brezhnev, and others who, being products of the party apparatus, have been permanently tied to its interests from the very start of their careers, and who have maintained their own positions of power only with the support of the very same apparatus. Leaders who methodically strove to achieve personal power and responded to the people's needs and interests only to the extent that these did not obstruct the pursuit of their own personal interests have therefore been unable to recognize any contradictions between the interests of the population and those of the party apparatus. Even when, as in the case of Stalin, they progressed beyond being a mere product of the party apparatus to the point of achieving an artificially created "popularity" with the people, they were well aware of the fact that this "popularity" had been created by the apparatus without whose support they would have been powerless to begin with.

When thinking of Lenin, however, we must say that this disposition was not typical of all communist leaders. Lenin has been described even by his many opponents and rivals as a person who did not think in terms of achieving personal power. Trotsky, who was the party leader most attacked by Lenin said of him: "Lenin highly valued power as an instrument of action, but struggling for power just for power's sake was totally foreign to him, unlike Stalin."[4]

Lenin therefore cannot be said to have been a power-hungry product of the party apparatus. His personal search for ways and means of promoting the interests of the working class can be called erroneous, simplified, or fanatical but not dishonest. But even Lenin had established limits that he himself was unable to cross. Being possibly the brightest theoretician and social analyst among all the communist leaders, he also was the sharpest critic of the bureaucracy and of the bureaucratization of the party, even after the communist takeover. As long as he lived, Lenin was honestly looking for ways and means of overcoming this terrible social phenomenon. According to Trotsky, he had even come to the conclusion that the cause of the bureaucratization had to be found in the party's organizational apparatus and in the position of its General Secretary.[5] However, he had not uncovered the real causes. As long as communist functionaries are monopolizing power and, independently of the working masses, are occupying attractive and influential positions within society that allow them to shape society's development, they will always band together to form a bureaucratic caste. Lenin did not live long enough to become aware of this fact. It will remain an unanswered question whether he really did not perceive the problem, for his criticism of the bureaucratized party functionaries during the last years of his life was exceedingly frequent and sharp. But to admit that this development necessarily resulted from an undemocratic one-party system would have meant for Lenin to negate his lifework as well as to exclude himself from the power elite that he himself had elevated to its exclusive social position. Here, therefore, was the limit of Lenin's publicly admitted perception of, and possibility to eliminate, the shortcomings that he himself had been criticizing.

After Lenin, none of the communist functionaries had the political power and the analytical mind to be able to address himself directly without the party's intermediary to the people in order to call for a change of the system that would have been adverse to the principle of the "leading role of the party." It is interesting to remember in this context that Khrushchev, although a typical representative of the party apparatus, in 1962 made a hardly publicized attempt to divide the party apparatus into two independent sections, one industrial and the other agricultural, each with its own secretariat and all the necessary services. Even though this reform would not have ended the party apparatus' supremacy, it might have allowed for a relatively more independent promotion of the needs and interests of the agricultural sector as opposed to the preference given to forced industrialization. Although Khrushchev's measures were problematic and uncoordinated (e.g., the elimination of the traditional system of economic ministries, the projected decentralization of the Gosplan, and so forth) and although these measures clearly were not intended to impair the leading role of the party, they were nevertheless a threat to the bureaucratic apparatus. The reforms threatened the monolithic hierarchy, the undebated promotion of its special interests, and the safeguard of its privileged positions. This was one of the main reasons why Khrushchev in the end lost the apparatus' support and was forced out of power.

Even more interesting is Mao Tse-tung's attempt to overcome the bureaucracy's despotism with the help of an antibureaucratic cultural revolution. It is the *unique attempt* of a communist leader to call on the working classes not only by passing over the head of the party apparatus but by actually opposing it with the aim of transforming both state and party apparatus. But at the same time it is the sign of a power struggle within the highest party organs where, with the apparatus' increasing support, Liu Shao-chi exercised a growing influence on the system's development. With the help of this new

social revolution Mao undoubtedly hoped to put a halt to a development of which he disapproved from an ideological point of view and
which also threatened his own powerful position. Mao reacted to the
apparent and automatic tendency of a growing segment of the
apparatus not to consider him its responsible representative any
longer.

It is not the object of this study to closely analyze specifically
Chinese problems but it seemed helpful to briefly describe the unique
process where a communist leader addressed himself to the people
even against the interest of the communist party apparatus. This
process originated on the one hand because a large segment of the
apparatus disassociated itself from Mao, and on the other hand
because of the tendency of Soviet foreign policy to support and
exploit the Chinese bureaucracy's opposition against Mao. Therefore, it was the overall situation that forced Mao to look for different
and efficient social support for his fight against the bureaucratic
apparatus. But even this unique action was not directed against the
principle of the leading role of the Communist Party or, in other
words, against the monopolistic political position of one party. The
primary cause for the growing bureaucratization of communist
functionaries had still not been removed.[6] But the characteristics of
the apparatus itself had remained unchanged in the process, and as
soon as the excitement of the cultural revolution had died down, the
apparatus restructured itself and recruited new members. In due
time this apparatus will have trained new bureaucrats and will
operate by applying more or less the same methods as before. Even a
succession of "cultural revolutions" cannot eliminate the bureaucratic phenomenon as long as certain basic traits of the system itself
have not been changed. It is, therefore, simply not reasonable to
expect the solution from the great leaders, even though some of them
actually recognized, criticized, and even tried, to eliminate this most
dangerous phenomenon. However, the fact must not be overlooked
that during the past development of communism within the Soviet
sphere of power the bureaucratic apparatus has brought forth
mainly leaders who did not turn against it but who, on the contrary,
became the most expressive proponents of its special interests.

This is not to say that the leaders, the key party officials, and the
general secretaries of the party in a communist country are not
interested in a well-functioning economy, or in raising their peoples'
living standard, or in a prosperous socialist system. This subjective
interest certainly does exist in the political leaders but it is only
secondary to their main interest, which is to maintain control of
everything and not to have their personal power jeopardized. Fur-

thermore, they will always be convinced that there is no contradiction between their interest in safeguarding their own political positions and the interests of society as a whole. In reality, however, such contradictions are bound to appear. For the possibilities of the rulers to recognize realistic facts do not always correspond to the needs of a developing society. On the contrary, beginning at a certain stage of development there can be conflict with newly emerging needs, since the choice of leaders (if there is choice) operated at a *certain stage of development* does not necessarily correspond to the requirements of a later and *qualitatively different stage.* This consideration alone should justify the democratic demand for a periodical change of party leaders, heads of government, and other officials. Only such change can guarantee that the most capable, the best prepared, and the most highly qualified men occupy the leading positions within a society. Those who master perfectly the tasks of revolutionary struggle are not necessarily experts in socialist economy. And to correctly grasp the problems of a certain stage of industrialization as well as of the corresponding extensive economic-political methods does not automatically imply a sufficient understanding of entirely new goals and measures of a period of expansion characterized by labor shortage and problems of efficiency. As long as the communist system does not allow for such an automatic change in leadership as well as for a genuinely free and public confrontation of differing views and the resulting initiative by various politicians and groups for alternative solutions, there will be serious and increasing difficulties in the process of development and considerable losses involved for society.

Even more dangerous than these shortcomings that communist leaders have to face after a longer reign and that lead to conflicts with their people are their special political interests, which do not allow for any changes liable to threaten this position of power. When a society has no real choice by means of elections, it has no possibility of controlling, criticizing, and—if necessary—dismissing its leaders by normal institutionally guaranteed means. When politicians are not responsible de facto to the people but rule autocratically, when everyone has to conform to the wishes of one person who with the support of a bureaucratic apparatus can decide which opinions are admissible and can be publicized, and which concepts can be recognized or have to be declared antagonistic, then such a situation automatically leads to a personification of "social" interests, to the identification of the ruler's interests with society's interests. This means that any opposing view or any proposal not corresponding to the ruler's personal interests has to be suppressed without society having a chance to examine alternatives and to decide if these alternatives would be more appropriate than those dictated by the leader.

The so-called principle of "collective leadership" that is often presented as an effective barrier to one-man rule is only a purely formalistic measure and does not touch on the essence of the problem. As long as the people are not able to elect, control, criticize and dismiss their leaders, "collective leadership" means nothing but priority of this group's interests over those of the people. In addition, within the group of leaders there will always be covert power struggles, imbalances, and fluctuations eventually resulting in the supremacy of one leader over the others. The real problem is then the existence of bureaucratic power supporting the personal power of the key functionaries.

It may seem that Stalin, Khrushchev, Brezhnev, or others retained real power and were able to promote their personal interests. However, there is a dialectical relation between the power of the key functionaries and the power of the bureaucratic party apparatus, with the first enjoying relatively great independence—according to the degree of their propagandistically exaggerated popularity—but the second exercising real power in the long run. As long as the First Secretary pursues more or less a policy corresponding to the basic interests of the party bureaucracy, he will be able to maintain his predominant position. But as soon as he attempts to initiate political changes directed against the party apparatus' interests, he is bound to fail sooner or later. This mechanism, which is typical of communist systems, could not be altered by Mao's unique action in any way, although at the time of his waning influence on the party apparatus he was still powerful enough to initiate a revolutionary movement against the bureaucracy.

In general, however, the bureaucracy as a whole is the leading, ruling, and deciding caste in the communist system, and without its support neither the individual leader nor a group of leaders can assert themselves over a long period of time. The bureaucracy is the best organized and, from the point of view of special interests, the most homogeneous social group within which the Communist Party bureaucracy plays the major role. Even though the party bureaucracy needs the entire bureaucratic state apparatus in order to dominate the people and therefore shares its basic interests, the party bureaucracy constitutes a power elite in relation to which the state bureaucracy assumes an inferior position.

The party bureaucracy has at its disposal such exclusive and complex information as well as the monopolistic instruments for manipulating people that the politician who has the support of this bureaucracy will be able to defeat all his rivals as long as the bureaucracy does not lose its own powerful position, for example in the course of revolutionary upheavals. Personal power struggles among key communist politicians have always been—and will always be—primarily fights for obtaining the decisive support of the party apparatus. In this context, it is not only important who among the politicians is closest to the current interests of the apparatus but it is equally important who through personal relationships manages to have on his side the greatest number of the most influential among the bureaucrats (party secretaries, department heads, and so forth). This may require years of preparation and systematically planned action.

In situations of open or covert personal power struggle, the politician who has thus become the most trusted representative of the party apparatus and who therefore benefits from its support will always be successful in fighting others or in maneuvering others into inferior positions. Inversely, the politician who does not or can no longer benefit from the party apparatus' support, or who attacks the apparatus' favorite representative, will almost certainly lose the battle. Trotsky and others had to experience this when trying to fight Stalin, just as Khrushchev had to become aware of this mechanism when he attempted to act against the interests of the apparatus, and Kosygin, too, when he had to give in to Brezhnev's actual supremacy. If Brezhnev ever was to forfeit the support of the party apparatus, he would experience the same fate as his predecessors. When Gomulka introduced his untimely wage and price policies that caused widespread acts of desperation among large segments of the working class and thereby threatened the party bureaucracy's position, he lost its support and had to resign in favor of Gierek, the party apparatus' new representative. Novotny would never have been removed from power had not the party apparatus felt increasing doubts about his rule and prepared for a change at the top. When, in addition, a revolutionary movement initiated changes at the top against the will of the majority of the party functionaries, the party apparatus itself became the reformers' greatest enemy and thus helped prepare external military intervention.

Even though in a communist system the political leaders will always play a much more important role than in a democratic system, both in their initial revolutionary as well as their later consolidating activities, this role can only be fully understood if we are aware of the specific mechanism of the "socialist" bureaucracy. Only in relation to this special interest group and its role within the system can the possibilities and tendencies of the leading personalities become more clearly understood.

GENERAL CHARACTERISTICS OF THE BUREAUCRACY

In order to fully understand the nature of communist bureaucracy it is necessary to analyze the specifically Soviet conditions and their origins on the basis of a general description of the problem of bureaucracy. Historically, the development of a bureaucracy and of its dominating position in society as an important instrument in the exercise of power of other social classes as well as of its own special interests is not new. The bureaucracy has always been subjected to the interests of the economically and politically most powerful classes but for short-lived exceptional situations when power was equally balanced among several rivaling classes, and when the bureaucracy temporarily became the strongest power in the state dominating these classes.[7] Only with the advent of the communist system in the Soviet Union and the simultaneous elimination of important internal and external antibureaucratic factors did the bureaucracy for the first time in history become the absolute power in a society. In order to understand this process, a general description of the bureaucracy's characteristics should be given.

I will try to describe in a brief generalization the position and role of the bureaucracy primarily in legal bourgeois systems of government and the specific activities, interests, and attitudes typical of their bureaucratic administrative apparatus.[8] At the same time, the limitations and the *antibureaucratic* elements, interests, and structures will become apparent; this will enable us to better understand the mechanism that applies in a communist system when due to the elimination of such antibureaucratic elements the position and role of the bureaucracy undergo essential changes. It will also demonstrate how various seemingly adverse bureaucratic tendencies that appear even in today's highly developed capitalistic states are being carried to their extremes, completely perverting the theoretically socialist system.

Generally speaking, a bureaucracy is the product of a division of labor within the society that has led to a separation of handicrafts from agriculture, to the growth of cities, the development of trade between town and countryside, and, finally, to a class structure and the formation of a state. This historical evolution has resulted in the development of complicated organizational activities and processes within the society, necessitating highly concentrated and complex decisions concerning the development of all these socialized activities and processes with the help of special and professional administrative organizations. Differently concentrated agglomerations of activities and interpersonal or interinstitutional relations also require differently extended, continuous, or periodical decision-making processes pertaining to the nature of these activities and relationships. All the related activities can generally be termed administrative activities: collection and evaluation of information, decision making and transmission of decisions, filing, surveillance, formulation, application and supervision of regulations, and so forth. In turn, these administrative activities necessitate the development of more or less extended administrative organizations, employing many professional officials and other employees, as well as a specific division of labor within this apparatus.

The largest administrative apparatuses were created as state apparatuses and are connected to the historical development of state-organized class societies. Therefore, to administrate always implies to exercise power and to rule, for an administration will always be tied to the pursuit of special political interests and to the issue of orders to be followed by a certain segment of the population. Any administration needs some degree of power, for in order to function some authority has to be placed into somebody's hand.[9] It follows that administrative activity can never be considered a purely rational activity based on the understanding of objective contexts and growth needs of the administrated human and institutional agglomerations, but that it will at the same time always represent an activity promoting special interests and possibly counteracting oppositional interests. Although "ruling," according to Max Weber, always implies "to find compliance to orders with a definable group of people,"[10] this does not mean that the *obeying* people automatically have the same interests as the *ruling* or that they always obey *happily and voluntarily*. Obedience that is obtained by "fear of the ruler's vengeance"[11] in authoritarian systems without identification of interests between governing and governed is a necessary condition for the exercise of power.

The terms "bureaucrat," designating the official of an administrative apparatus, and "bureaucracy," referring to the entire social group, have always had a derogatory connotation that reflects the various negative characteristics of this administrative activity.[12] Not many other human activities are as contradictory as administrating. Its basic function is the administration of those activities and processes required by society that could not be carried out in an organized fashion without this administration. Simultaneously, there will always be negative effects that are defined by the word "bureaucratism": the pursuit of goals corresponding to specific interests not shared by the population as a whole, and an excessively formalized process of administrative activities characterized by increasing inefficiency. In case of excessive dimensions of the apparatus as well as under specific social conditions, this negative aspect of administrative activity can reach proportions that may seriously impair the positive aspects and make the overall image appear more negative than positive. Under certain conditions and especially in the Soviet version of communism, the negative impact on large segments of the population can become unbearable to an extent that it is important to carefully examine the characteristics and origins of the negative aspects of administrative systems, that is, of bureaucratism as such.

This is not to say that the positive, socially beneficial aspect of administrative activity has to be neglected. Even the anarchistic critics of state bureaucracy, like Proudhon, Bakunin, Kropotkin, and others have not denied the necessity of social administrative activity itself but have described only the negative function of state and bureaucracy and have tried to find solutions for overcoming this aspect. Criticism of the atypical power concentration and repressive function of the state has led them to oppose and to fight the state organization as such and to recommend various forms of self-government.

A professional state administration has the general, socially required—and therefore positive—function of coordinating a practically unlimited amount of activities created by division of labor within a more or less extended national territory. Furthermore, the state administration has to establish legal modes of behavior as well as the necessary material conditions for their application and to protect these from internal and external aggression. It is obvious that a society which is highly developed in terms of productivity and division of labor requires professional administrative activity, for it is hardly conceivable at the present stage of development that an administration could function without a specific apparatus of officials. However, it is possible to conceive of differences in the conduct of administrative activities, in its internal organization, its efficiency, the process of decision making within the administrative apparatus, its subordination to special interests in a multi-interest society, the ways and means of furthering interests and of executing decisions. Under certain social conditions and at certain historical periods, all these factors may have a varyingly strong positive or negative impact on the development of a state-organized society. Since the term "bureaucratism" primarily designates an administration's negative forms of manifestation, I will concentrate here on the analysis of this particular aspect.

Another reason for not having to dwell too much on the beneficial aspect of administrative activity is that Max Weber has dealt very authoritatively with this issue. However, Weber's explanation of the advantages of bureaucratic activity is probably a one-sided apology just as the anarchistic interpretation is a one-sided condemnation of its negative manifestations. When Weber describes the advantages of the bureaucratic organization as compared to other nonbureaucratic administrative activities, for example, he does not take into account the fact that these "advantages" do not appear equally advantageous to all classes and social strata alike, that the bureaucratic activity therefore has a different significance for different people within a class-structured society. From this point of view, every one of its characteristic traits can be both accepted and rejected, a fact which makes it necessary at least to relativize Weber's predominantly positive evaluation. "Precision, rapidity, clarity, unity, subordination, a minimum of frictions, of material and personal costs"[13] are Weber's characteristics of the advantages of bureaucratic organization. Compared to an amateur, untrained, and part-time administrative activity, these criteria are acceptable, though only with certain reservations. I will point out below the opposite elements that are equally important and under certain conditions justify the search for essential changes in the state administrative system and several of its organizational principles.

If we see the socially useful aspect of professional officialdom in the fact that it allows for coordination and control of complicated and diversified highly socialized activities—and very possibly more efficiently than in the case of "part-time" administration—then the negative, that is, bureaucratic manifestation of administrative activity can be divided into two specific series of issues. The first concerns the evaluation of those special interests that are hiding behind the bureaucratic activity or, in other words, whose purpose it serves. The second refers to the more detailed knowledge of the imminently important limitations and shortcomings of inefficient bureaucratic activity that occur under certain circumstances. We shall have to look more closely at these problems.

As long as society is divided into classes and social strata with differing or opposing interests, and as long as politics is a power struggle between special interest groups, the state as a complex of the most important instruments of power will always be more useful to some special interest groups than to others. This is not in contradiction to the practically neutral function of a state placed above group interests that is required in order to channel conflicts of interests and to secure their solution within the limits of a generally accepted legal order.[14] In fact, special interest groups exist even in the modern democratic state that formally functions as guardian of the legal equality of all its citizens. The fact alone that laws are always laid down in a certain situation when the economically and politically most powerful special interest groups have a decisive influence on legislation implies that laws correspond to some interests more than to others. It is not only a question of the basic Marxist theory that the economically most powerful classes, the classes of the owners of the means of production, that is, the proprietors, will always benefit more than the propertyless from those basic rights that are intended to guarantee the established ownership system. Even Weber had to acknowledge this mechanism: "In particular, the propertyless masses do not benefit from formal 'equal rights' and a 'predictable' jurisdiction and administration called for by 'bourgeois' interests. For them, law and administration by definition have to serve the purpose of equalizing economic and social chances in relation to the property-owning classes. However, they will only be able to perform this function if they appear as informal and 'ethical' in character."[15]

But not only certain basic rights that are intended to safeguard existing ownership conditions and are therefore differently significant for property-owning classes and for propertyless classes are designed by governments—and by the special interests that are backing them—to more or less neglect the interests of the opponents. The majority of all other laws and regulations as well serve the same purpose and are bound to be biased. Besides, the interpretation and enforcement of laws and regulations invariably allow for a certain flexibility in addition to the freedom of action within the framework of general economic and other legislation. All this implies, however, that in reality the supposedly interest-free activity of states always is, and has to be, an interest-preferring activity as long as essentially differing group interests and conflicts of interests do exist.

In cases where the state bureaucracy is even one of the decisive elements in the entire state machinery, its activity will have a different impact on the different social classes, the more so if the bureaucracy is consistent as to the observation of its laws and regulations. The larger the segment of the population that due to the political situation is unable to promote its special interests, the stronger the opposition against the bureaucratic activity which as a symbol of pressure is endured with growing resentment and can even lead to open rebellion by social groups with essentially different interests.

Although the bureaucracy has always exerted an influence on the actual legal structure of states and of their various forms of activities, its role in all social orders until the establishment of the communist system has been that of an instrument of more powerful special interests backing the political power. The bureaucrats may have marked the state machinery but they were themselves prisoners of this power. The more they identified with this power, the less they were aware of their own position as prisoners, but the more they were hated as representatives of this power.[16] However, the more power one wields, the less one feels hatred; the higher one is placed, the more one meets with submissiveness from subordinates and with respect from the ordinary people. The more the bureaucracy appears as the personification of power, the greater the estrangement from the people and the stronger the incentive to develop specifically bureaucratic interests.

The primary interest of any bureaucracy is to maintain and to extend the bureaucratic apparatus. The existence of the apparatus is the precondition for a promotion of the specific economical and political interests of the bureaucracy. The economic interest of the bureaucrats concentrates on their salary (in developing countries also on baksheesh and other bribes). The scale of salaries—and bribes—in a hierarchically organized system of state officials creates a strong drive for promotion and stimulates excessive career-thinking.

The continuous exercise of a bureaucratic activity whose basic aim is to help exercise authority puts the bureaucrat in a position of power in relation to the ordinary citizen. Regulations and orders; controlling and forbidding; setting up forms and taking decisions; supervising, threatening, harassing and censuring become the exclusive activity of, and a career for, certain people.[17] With many bureaucrats, the exercise of such "sovereign" activity creates a certain satisfaction and a feeling of self-worth that through repetition and extension is liable to develop into a specific interest in the power of bureaucracy. The bureaucratic interest in power is not necessarily tied only to an economic interest but can under certain circumstances develop into an even more powerful incentive for action. The more extensive a bureaucratic apparatus becomes and the more people it employs, the better the chances for the individual bureaucrat to move up into a higher salary bracket, to see his position strengthened and his functions extended. This explains the tendency typical of all bureaucracies to extend the range of bureaucratic activities, to artificially create the need for new studies, evaluations, proposals, regulations, information sheets, files, and so forth. The amount of bureaucratic activities grows faster than the amount of activities that are controlled by the bureaucracy, as C. N. Parkinson has so clearly demonstrated.[18] Each senior bureaucrat will try to have more and more new collaborators under his orders since this automatically extends his range of power.

The specific bureaucratic interest in power and income is bound to be in contradiction with the interests of the rest of the population. It is a contradiction between the mass of the people who have to obey and the minority who have the means of enforcing obedience. This relationship is liable to create tension even if the obedient citizens identify with the interests as expressed by bureaucratic regulations. In those segments of the population that oppose certain legally determined goals, the bureaucratic way of enforcing these interests will create strong frustrations. If, in addition, the material security of the bureaucracy is ensured by taxes, an economic conflict is added to the power conflict.

The special interests of the bureaucracy together with a number of other factors are creating a specific kind of bureaucratic activity that further contributes to a negative judgment on the part of the population. A specific division of labor necessarily evolves within the big bureaucratic apparatus. The greater the amount of evaluations, decisions, regulations, studies, information processing and controls, and the more sections and divisions to administer, the greater the number of officials who can be provided with work. If to this is added—as has been mentioned above—the specific bureaucratic interest in a maximum extension of the apparatus, the division of labor proceeds to a degree where concentration and synthetization become increasingly difficult to implement. The activities of the individual bureaucrat as well as of certain sections tend to be self-generating, which basically is the sign of a loss of oversight of realistic interrelationships within the intricate complex of administered activities. In their hierarchical structure of superior and inferior positions, individual divisions, sections, and offices are no longer able to see the indirect consequences of their decisions in spheres of action other than their own. In the same way they are not in a position to evaluate or to change the impact of another administration's decision on their own subordinated sections. The resulting administrative division of labor leads to a growing inefficiency of the administrative apparatus and has an adverse influence on all administrated activities. Purely mechanical, inappropriate, and untimely decisions and regulations are visible proof of a lack of understanding of real life and of a self-generating bureaucratic activity. The more the internal development becomes an end in itself, the more important are files, forms, and all the other paper paraphernalia. The result is that dreadful atmosphere of pettiness and office routine in which administrative forms take on real life, and real life becomes a mere reflection of forms.[19] The apparatus becomes self-sufficient, its value judgments are vital for the bureaucrat, and the "customer" is considered a time-wasting nuisance interfering with his schedule. Dutifulness and discipline are elevated to supreme bureaucratic law at the cost of human emotions, but they ensure a safe road to a successful career.

"The observation of rules, originally a means, becomes an end in itself; this results in the well-known process of goal-shifting, whereby an 'instrumental value becomes the final value.' Easily interpreted as loyalty to regulations under any circumstances, discipline is not understood by the bureaucrat as a means to meet certain ends but becomes a value factor for his way of life. The stress on discipline as a result of a shifting away from the original goals leads to rigidity and to the incapacity of being flexible and able to adjust. Formalism and even ritualism are the consequences of unchangeable persistence on excessively formalized modes of behavior."[20]

For the inferior services all directives and orders coming from above are an expression of the omniscience of the supreme power that instills even in the lowest placed official a feeling of playing an essential part in the countinued existence of the state. Be he emperor or party chief, for the bureaucrat the head of state's unquestioned knowledge of what is necessary for the government is a protective shield against any criticism in the exercise of his functions. For their part, both emperor and party chief rely on the information supplied by their bureaucrats[21] to whom they have officially delegated the precise understanding of society's problems. The state administration's officials are the mouthpiece of the people and the liaison between people and government. Whatever the functionaries have not reported does not exist. But since information from the base is filtered on its way up and, by generalizing, is made to conform to regulations and to bureaucratic conventionalism, the final result will be misinformation reflecting the bureaucrats' attitude toward life.

The less efficient the bureaucratic activity, the more there will be formalism and unrealistic regulations; the stronger the feeling of repulsion in the population, the more determined the defense of bureaucratic authority! The absolute knowledge of the bureaucracy must not be contested, for its superiority over the ordinary citizen's intelligence has been established by law. "Therefore, authority is the principle of their knowledge, and deification of authority their way of thinking."[22] The skeptic antiauthoritarian will be branded an archenemy by the emperor's officials and by the party apparatus' bosses alike.

In order to protect the bureaucratic apparatus from any criticism and to keep the appearance of an infallible and objective governmental and administrative activity "in the exclusive service of the people," this activity has to be shrouded by a veil of secrecy.[23] The czarist as well as the communist body of power have always been comfortable in wearing the cloak of secrecy and impenetrability that conceals so well the real interests behind decisions and orders, the ignorance of real life and the inefficiency of endless meetings and agendas, the competition and infights among departments, sections and services, the career-promoting plots, the rumor-spreading, and spying on nonconformist individuals. "The General Spirit of bureaucracy is the secret, the mystery which it protects internally by creating a hierarchy, and externally by forming a closed corporation."[24]

If we examine the internal and external factors that substantially curtail the development of bureaucratic characteristics in an administration, we have to mention as an internal factor mainly the *market interests of the officials*, and as an external factor *democratic political conditions*.

Market interests here refer to those activities of control and administration that are primarily related to the production and sale of goods (material goods and services). This obviously excludes the state administrative apparatus and concerns those in the economic sector. The specific trait of economy-oriented administrative activity is that the *outcome* of this activity becomes visible in the *market results* and that remunerations depend directly on these results. Whereas in most cases the results of state and similar administrative activities cannot be sold in the market and therefore the efficiency is hardly measurable, in the sectors of production and trade administrative expenses enter into the cost evaluation of the finished products, thus being in immediate quantitative relation to the overall profits made on the sold goods. The relatively smaller the administrative costs or the higher the proceeds in relation to these costs are, the more efficient is the administrative activity.

Since the administration in the economic sector has an essential impact on the quantitative development of production and trade activities it will be all the more efficient the higher the overall profits in relation to its own costs and those incurred by production and trade. The fact alone that the administrative activity in the economic sector can be measured makes it possible for the businessman to evaluate its efficiency. Continuous comparisons with competitors makes it immediately evident if the administrative apparatus is too big, that is, less efficient, or if it is adequate. On this basis, administrative efficiency can then be improved by hiring better qualified employees and by introducing better organization and mechanization within the administration. Also, it is then possible to eliminate bureaucratic tendencies that aim at extending the apparatus for the sake of extension. If, in addition, the officials' income is partially tied to the profit (profit sharing, bonuses, and similar schemes), thus creating a personal interest in maximum efficiency, the tendencies toward bureaucratization will be curtailed even more effectively.

However, the fact cannot be denied entirely that with the

development of very extensive and highly concentrated or greatly diversified corporations there are bound to be, even in the economic sector, huge administrations with tendencies toward bureaucratization. In such a big apparatus, the efficiency assessment of administrative activities will be more difficult because the apparatus itself becomes increasingly complex and therefore its efficiency will be less easy to compare with that of competing enterprises. With growing monopolization and with increasing profits and simultaneously decreasing competitive pressure, administrative efficiency becomes more difficult to assess and to compare. At the same time, we observe an increasing bureaucratization. Very often the possibilities of directly linking employees' income to the company's profits are reduced. Contacts between the central administrative apparatus and an increasing number of production, sales, and other services tend to become less direct and therefore less liable to stimulate the interest of employees in the efficiency of the entire enterprise.

However, despite these tendencies the efficiency of the administrative apparatus in the economic sector can nevertheless be assessed and controlled, and the officials' interest in efficiency is markedly greater than in the state apparatus. This is the reason why bureaucratization is much less developed here than in the state apparatus, and it is this last type of administration that is mostly being referred to with the term "bureaucratism." Besides, the economic apparatus does not aim at promoting political but economic interests, which makes an essential difference in the methods of administration. The typical excesses of an uncontrollable power apparatus—such as red tape, artificially inflated agendas, extensive research and controls, manifestations of prestige behavior, and persecution of enemies—can hardly occur in a market-oriented company. In the economic sector, the socially useful content of administrative activity is not negated by tendencies toward bureaucratization as is the case in the state apparatus and similar administrations under certain circumstances. If we use the term "bureaucracy" in the sociological sense, that is, to describe a specific social group within the societal structure, we should apply this definition to the state functionaries or officials of other political apparatus (party and the like) and distinguish this social group as a matter of principle from the administrative and technical-economic employees in a market-economy business.

As long as the activity of functionaries is directly linked to economic efficiency and can be evaluated and remunerated accordingly, this activity itself will not develop into a power-oriented end in itself, nor into an exaggerated make-believe activity. The rational assessment of production and trade activities in possibly all its aspects, the striving for maximum efficiency, and the obtainment of optimal results are characteristic of a market-oriented administration. As soon as the direct link of administrative activity to market achievement begins to disappear, the character of rationality, too, gradually fades away while the process of bureaucratization takes over. One of the essential differences between state and economic administration is the difficulty, and in many sectors the impossibility, of establishing a direct link between the state and general political administration (its evaluation and remuneration) on the one side and, on the other side, certain market criteria, that is, input-output relations which result from market prices and competitive conditions.

To take an example, when not only private owners but also profit-sharing employees of market enterprises have to decide on investment projects, the decision-making process will greatly differ from the routine followed by a commission of state functionaries even if the commission consists of so-called experts. The person who knows that his own future income depends significantly on the investment he decides on today will demonstrate his involvement by using all available information and by acting in full understanding of his personal responsibility.

The commission of functionaries, too, will make an effort to use available information but personal commitment and responsibility will be missing in the actual decision making. Economically disinterested, the bureaucrats will discuss a project for one, two, or maybe three days but after the presentation of the different arguments and after long and exhausting discussions, each participant will be trying to have the commission reach its decision as rapidly as possible. Everyone is aware of the fact that should the decision prove wrong none of the commission's members can later be made responsible and none of them will have to suffer any economic losses.

The greater the number of economic processes that reach beyond the enterprises's scope of decision and that are influenced by economically disinterested state officials, the more probable it is that a gradual bureaucratization of the entire economy will take place. The reasons are obvious: an expanding state-administered and state-controlled infrastructure requires an increasing regulation of construction, environment protection, quality and price control, health care, and transport. There will be more industrial state enterprises; an increase in anticyclical and antiinflationary measures and directives; more closely regulated labor conditions; substantial state activities in the social, medical, cultural, and educational sectors; and, consequently, an increasingly important role for the state in the redistribution of income. Logically, the amount of bureaucratic activities increases accordingly: more studies, meetings, question-naires, forms, directives, controls, inquiries, admonitions, summons, and so forth. The ensuing problems of coordinating interrelated processes result in a multitude of contradictions, mistakes, losses, and serious inconveniences, not to mention all those bureaucratic decisions that are taken on the basis of political or ideological interests and are bound to be in contradiction with the interests of large segments of the population.

With the increase in the amount of activities by the state, bureaucracy begins, in a democracy, the search for ways and means to methodically limit centralized decision making (decentralization), to consider economic criteria to the largest possible extent, to increase and intensify democratic and public control, and to replace detailed centralized decision making by global goal-setting and overall planning. However, these efforts can only succeed under democratic conditions when large segments of the population—those suffering most from the consequences of bureaucratic administra-tion—have at least the possibility of fighting the growing bureau-cratization of society. This leads us to the external antibureaucratic element.

Democratic societies, too, at certain times had a need for further and more far-reaching democratization,[25] especially when existing democratic systems became increasingly formal, thus complicating the effective promotion of the people's interests and creating an even greater lack of understanding of the state's activities on the part of the population. Whether we look at a totalitarian or at a democratic system, the gap existing between the state and the ordinary citizen has always been linked to the state's growing bureaucratization and to the exploitation of the people by relatively limited but powerful special interest groups, even though there is an important difference of degree in estrangement between totalitarian and democratic systems. Therefore, the struggle for an extension and intensification of democracy has always been at the same time a fight for limiting the powers of bureaucracy, for gaining more influence and control over its activities by larger segments of the population, for creating new and more efficient systems of decision making, and administrat-ing in the service of the people.

One of the characteristics of democratic systems is the fact that the mass of administrated individuals has certain means of exerting political pressure in order to curtail excessive bureaucratic power. It is important to remember that within a pluralistic democracy there always exists competition between the differing bureaucratic party apparatuses that helps prevent a monopolization of the state bu-reaucracy. By means of competitive political alternatives for various procedures of administration and control, specific bureaucratic interests and modes of behavior can be more easily detected and limited.

If democratic procedures are eliminated in a capitalist state (e.g., in a fascist system), thus leading to a monopolization of the party bureaucracy and consequently of the state bureaucracy, the specific interests of the party bureaucracy will basically be identical with those of big business. At the same time, however, there can be a conflict of interests concerning various partial goals or specific actions. But in a fascist system, the bureaucracy on the whole remains subordinated to the basic interests of big business and does not develop into an absolute political power even though bureaucratic behavior toward the people may take intolerable forms.

The social content of democratic systems of government may differ from one to the other but, in contrast to totalitarian systems, there is the possibility of resisting bureaucratic nonsense, pettiness, persecution, and repression. There is room, especially to fight legally and publicly in a democratic way for achieving further antibureaucratization and for enforcing more advanced reforms of the system.

The bureaucratic apparatus, however, will automatically oppose any attempts at democratization whatever the political system. In addition, it will attempt to obtain a limitation and formalization even of the verbal pledge for democracy of democratic governments "in the interests of the state." As there is no true democracy but only a permanent struggle by the people for freedom and rights in order to help promote genuine popular interests, the fight for democracy has always been a fight against bureaucratic omnipotence. Claiming to know the people's "real" interests, the bureaucracy has always considered itself the only authorized representative and guardian of the people. The bureaucracy will fight any control coming from below because it would undermine its powerful position based on secret information. As Weber[26] has stated:

> The power position of a fully developed bureaucracy is always great, under normal conditions overpowering. The political "master" always finds himself, vis-à-vis the trained official, in the position of a dilettante facing the expert. This holds whether the "master," whom the bureaucracy serves, is the "people" equipped with the weapons of legislative initiative, referendum, and the right to remove officials; or a parliament elected on a more aristocratic or more democratic basis and equipped with the right or the de facto power to vote a lack of confidence; or an aristocratic collegiate body, legally or actually based on self-recruitment; or a popularly elected president; or an "absolute" or "constitutional" hereditary monarch.[26]

The powerful position of the bureaucracy is not influenced by the fact that it has to serve differing class interests in differing socioeconomic systems and that, as a state bureaucracy, it can never act against the major interests of the economically and politically most powerful class. Whether it served the feudal aristocracy or the bourgeois merchants, the landed estates or capitalist industry, the bureaucracy at all times had sufficient, free scope of action to be able to make its own decisions and to exercise its legally protected arbitrary powers. While respecting the basic interests of the ruling class and the position of the richest and most powerful families, the bureaucracy dominated the entire administrative activity following the dictates of its own special interests.

This, of course, had its immediate effect on the broad masses of the population. Only in those political systems where democratic conditions allow for various public means of pressure can the people succeed somewhat in curtailing the bureaucracy's arbitrary power, i.e., in the ancient democracies of the slave states (excluding the slaves, of course) or in the bourgeois democracy. To a limited extent, this can also be achieved by certain election processes—limited because all elected representatives eventually will become dependent on the bureaucracy and on its monopoly of information, no matter which party they belong to, or what kind of parliamentarian democracy they live in.[27]

The possibility alone, however, to be able to freely set up political organizations and to elect representatives of differing political parties provides the people with a means of pressure against bureaucratic dominance. Evidently, this kind of pressure is not powerful enough to eliminate a given socioeconomic system and its established social structure and bureaucratic machinery, but in contrast to totalitarian states it enables the people to be better informed, to freely discuss the available information, to take initiative, and to consider and politically prepare essential social reforms.

Public opinion as expressed with the help of relatively liberal and progressive mass media can be even more effective than elections. In a democratic system, the bureaucracy does not have the possibility, as it does in communist systems, to suppress all criticism of its actions and to brand its critics as state enemies. In a country where the bureaucracy dominates the information and publication sector, where it can bend the truth and make black look white, where it cannot afford to publicly admit any nonconformist opinion but has the means of propagating its bureaucratic power goals under the cover of social interest, there is no possibility for public opinion to limit arbitrary bureaucratic power. However, the possibility given in a democracy to fight excessive administrative behavior with public criticism and exposure represents a limitation of bureaucratic power that should not be underestimated even though it will not be able to break this power. The implication will become clear when we study the communist system.

It is interesting to recall Weber's prediction on the bureaucratization in a communist economy that he made before the October Revolution in Russia.

> Wherever the modern specialized official comes to dominate, his power proves practically indestructible since the whole organization of even the most elementary has been tailored to his mode of operation. A progressive elimination of private capitalism is theoretically conceivable, although it is surely not so easy as imagined in the dreams of some liberati who do not know what it is all about. But let us assume that some time in the future it will be done away with. What would be the practical result? The destruction of the steel frame of modern industrial work? No! The abolition of private capitalism would simply mean that also the top management of the nationalized or socialized enterprises would become bureaucratic. Are the daily working conditions of the salaried employees and the workers in the state-owned Prussian mines and railroads really perceptibly different from those in big business enterprises? It is true that there is even less freedom, since every power struggle with a state bureaucracy is hopeless and since there is no appeal to an agency which as a matter of principle would be interested in limiting the employer's power, such as there is in the case of a private enterprise. That would be the whole difference. State bureaucracy would rule alone if private capitalism were eliminated. The private and public bureaucracies, which now work next to, and potentially against, each other and hence check one another to a degree, would be merged into a single hierarchy. This would be similar to the situation in ancient Egypt, but it would occur in a much more rational—and hence unbreakable—form.[28]

In conclusion, the following is a summary list of the negative interests and modes of behavior typical of a bureaucracy that in a bourgeois democracy can only occur in the form of limited tendencies. We have to stress primarily those tendencies that are not only typical in any politically monopolized bureaucracy—and mainly the specifically communist bureaucracy—but that appear under special conditions, in very marked, and partly absolutized, forms:

1. Interests of the bureaucrats in their careers and in the exercise of power. Consequently, major interest in consolidating and extending the bureaucratic apparatus and in fighting any changes that would limit the power of the bureaucracy.

2. Strict discipline in the exercise of bureaucratic functions and purely formal execution of orders and regulations according to hierarchical structures become an end in itself. Coordinated and authoritarian behavior toward the ordinary citizen.

3. Growing estrangement between the bureaucracy and the people due to the specific characteristics of the bureaucratic administration apparatus: exercise of power, special interests, exclusiveness of knowledge and information secrecy, economic privileges, authoritarian claims to prestige, formal procedures, and so forth.

4. Groupings and intrigues within the bureaucracy resulting primarily from power struggles among key functionaries, but without disrupting coordinated actions in dealing with the people.

5. Anonymity in decision making and, consequently, no assumption of responsibility toward the people. Public criticism aimed primarily at politicians generally gets lost in the jungle of bureaucratic regulations and alibis.

6. Nonexistence of material interests in economic decision making since economic profits or losses have no direct impact on the salaries of state bureaucrats. Bureaucratic control of production leads to increasing losses due to inefficiency.

THE SPECIFIC STRUCTURE OF THE BUREAUCRACY IN COMMUNIST SYSTEMS

The elimination of the internal and external antibureaucratic factors in the Soviet version of a communist system—which eliminated the subordination of the bureaucracy under the power of the capitalist class by liquidating private capital—did not only result in the creation of a *very large bureaucratic class dominating the entire economy* and *in an unprecedented inefficiency of its activity* but, primarily, in the *monopolization of power in the hands of a party bureaucracy.* Similar to what had happened in the past in various exceptional situations, a specific party bureaucracy has been evolving to become an absolute political power for an entire era of development, a power which is actually exercised with the help of an extended and subordinated state and economic apparatus.[29] Neither the working class nor any other social class or stratum of Soviet society can impose its interests and its will on the party bureaucracy. On the contrary, the bureaucracy takes into account other interests only to the extent that these interests coincide with its own interests. This is one of the *decisive characteristics of the Soviet communist bureaucratic development.*

From our earlier description of the Stalinist system in the Soviet Union and its development, it became quite obvious that party and state bureaucracy were not dedicated to the interests of the workers and peasants but that, on the contrary, only those political opinions and proposals had a chance to be considered that corresponded to the interests of the party apparatus. We will now show in a contracted and generalized way why in contrast to previous societal formations the bureaucracy could, first, expand quantitatively to such an extent and, second, could evolve into becoming the real monopolistic power ruling over the entire population. To state this in more general terms, under what conditions can a system develop that only promotes specifically bureaucratic interests and not those of the majority of the people?

We have seen that it is not at all important from which social classes and strata the bureaucrats originate and which kind of political, ideological, religious, or other conscience they were endowed with before they became officials. Although the Bolsheviks in Russia methodically destroyed the existing state apparatus and replaced most of the former czarist officials with sons of workers and peasants, and although their newly established party apparatus was made up of the most reliable among the communist revolutionaries, all these officials within a short time had become bureaucrats pursuing their own interests and showing typical bureaucratic modes of behavior. Even the most reliable of the Bolshevik fighters among whom the leading members of the party apparatus had been recruited have sooner or later turned into bureaucrats who were not only feared but also hated by the population because they behaved as if they were actually the ruling class. It became more obvious than ever that people's specific interests and goals, their modes of behavior, and their isolation and differentiation as a special group from other social groups are primarily a result of specific conditions due to work, income, and way of life. Although Marx had been fully aware of this principle, Lenin had failed to recognize this fact, and all his followers have refused to admit it.

Two decisive factors have been ignored in Marxist theory and especially in communist practice. Properly understood and recognized, both these factors would have helped curtail the emergence of bureaucratic supremacy. First, the significance of *real efficiency* of human activity for society and its *remuneration according to efficiency* has not been taken into consideration. This economic process was greatly simplified and has remained unsolved in communist practice. Second, the *differentiation of interests* even in a socialist society as well as the necessity of *democratic conditions* for an authentic *manifestation and promotion of popular interests* were not acknowledged.

At first, this problem was not understood and, later, no one was willing to understand it. Basically, there was a lack of understanding as well as a deliberate disregard of the internal and external antibureaucratic factors.

Let us take a look at the first issue. Primarily, it concerns the assessment of human activity for the benefit of society, not in a simplified way but in all its complexity and seen in the context of the necessity to appropriately remunerate labor according to its social effectiveness. Also, it implies the possibility of objective evaluation and appreciation of labor effectiveness as a condition for appropriate remuneration. It will become evident that the lack of full understanding and the neglect of these problems have resulted in the bureaucratization of the entire communist economic administration that necessarily led to an expansion of bureaucratic power unprecedented in all previous social systems.

The simplification of the concept of "labor" is mainly due to the fact that labor was understood to mean exclusively an output of human work. According to this interpretation, in Soviet economic practice only the quantity of labor contributed by working individuals (that is, energy actually spent at work), and the quality of labor as an expression of differing qualifications are evaluated and remunerated. It is assumed that the remuneration of different amounts of work (addressed directly by means of time spent on the job or, indirectly, on the basis of the quantity of goods produced or any other kind of output of labor) and of differing qualifications of labor (by categorizing the work force and establishing a scale of qualifications) corresponds to the socialist requirement of remunerating labor according to the work performed.

In reality, essential aspects of labor and of its social value and efficiency are thus being ignored or neglected. For it is decisive that labor supplies goods which actually fulfill society's needs and therefore represent socially required economic values. In a developed industrial economy, such values will not be provided by individual workers but by entire enterprise collectives. However, all members of this collective will have to be remunerated not only on the basis of a mechanically measured quantity and quality of work but also in view of the actual economic value produced for the benefit of society. Only this will guarantee the collective's sufficient and genuine interest in a socially required production.

However, this implies that in the case of a large amount of different kinds of goods produced by a big socialist enterprise collective (millions or even tens of millions of different products) all these different kinds of goods will have to be produced in the socially required quantities, that is, in proportion to society's needs, and with maximum quality development. It also means that all these goods have to be produced with maximum labor productivity and highly efficient exploitation of all production factors. Finally, a maximum innovation not only of goods and production techniques but also of the production organization will be indispensable. All these aspects of labor as supplied by a production collective have to be evaluated and remumerated if labor is to develop according to societal requirements.

If it is assumed that all these aspects of production—its maximum structural, proportional, qualitative, economical, and innovative development—are guaranteed first by central planning and second by decision making at the level of the sector or enterprise administration, and that, furthermore, it will be sufficient to pay the workers of the enterprise only according to the quantity and quality of their work, we have to call this assumption one of the basic fictions to which communist practice has fallen victim. Neither the central planning organism nor the economic ministries in charge of the various sectors are able to determine, plan, and supervise all the complicated aspects of production development in a large number of subordinated enterprises. In practice, they have to limit themselves to fixing global growth rates and to specifying a few priority tasks within these limits. Everything else, that is, all the above-mentioned essential aspects of production development are either left to the exclusive decision of the enterprise management or are incorporated in the plan on the basis of information supplied by the enterprises themselves.

However, management has to make decisions under conditions that do not allow for objectivity due to the lack of any market mechanism. By eliminating market prices, competition, and remuneration computed in relation to real market results, not only has the basic information needed for maximum production decisions disappeared but also the decisive interest of management in an efficient development of the production, trade, and administration of the enterprise. The nonexistence of real competition makes it impossible to assess whether an enterprise's management has made its decisions based on maximum consideration of the structural, proportional, qualitative, and economical factors within a specific sector, or if it could have done better. Since there are no free-market prices and no competitive pressure (not even a potential competition), there is no increase or decrease in income for management in relation to more or less effective production decisions, or to a more or less efficient production development. This means that the internal antibureaucratic factor has been removed and that the path is free for the unlimited bureaucratization of the enterprise's internal administrative activity, which will never be overcome by any kind of moral request nor by any amount of political mobilization.

The administration of an enterprise, however, does not only decide and control subjectively without taking into account objective competitive factors or at least the potential threat of competition. In addition, management is obliged to pursue and attain its quantitatively fixed results under the pressure of achieving the simplified growth rates as established by the central plans, since their fulfillment determines the payment of the planned wages and bonuses. This pressure is bound to negatively influence the qualitative and economic development of production. Very often a quantitative development is achieved in a purely fictitious way with the help of structural and price-related biases in the production statistics, to the detriment of the consumer, resulting in an economy like that of wartime, characterized by permanent shortages and by technical backwardness, as compared to capitalism.[30]

It goes without saying that the absence of any objective means of measuring the efficiency of enterprise and supraenterprise administration as well as the elimination of market interests on the part of the employed officials has two specific consequences: the bureaucratic idleness in the administrative apparatus is steadily growing, and the promotion of purely bureaucratic interests is increasingly difficult to control. Each official strives to expand his agenda, to multiply research and controls, and to make planning an end in itself. Since there are no objective criteria allowing for a limitation of these tendencies, they constitute the best means for establishing the bureaucrat's indispensability and for securing his career.

In this way, the entire economic administration develops into a bureaucratic Moloch. Priority is not given to rational considerations in view of a maximum cost reduction of production factors and a qualitative development of technology and output. Instead, wasteful planning and appointment agenda develop into a bureaucratic end in itself that reaches unprecedented dimensions: there are reports to be filed to the superior branch ministry; planning forms, plan fulfillment forms, and statistical questionnaires have to be filled in; prices have to be examined and listed, material has to be ordered and distributed, and labor force to be requested. There are forms to be filled in for the Ministry of Technology, for the Control of Product Quality, for the Central Bank, for the Ministry of Foreign Trade. There are reports on efficiency to be addressed to the party organs, there is production of papers and files, much pseudoactivity, and waste of time. The official agenda becomes the very content of bureaucratic activity, and the real content of productive results becomes a secondary goal. The faster the bureaucracy grows and the bigger the management and administration apparatuses become, the greater are the career opportunities for the individual official, the increase in his remuneration, and the scope of his functions. The automatism of bureaucratic self-generation results in a much more rapid growth of the supraenterprise administration apparatus than of the employment in the production enterprises and of production itself.

This situation is clearly demonstrated in Table 1 which shows the increase in expenses for the central administrative apparatus in relation to the growth rate in production and labor force in the enterprises in a few selected sectors of the Soviet economy between 1966 and 1968 (in percent for 1968 on the basis of 1966 = 100 percent).

In the hierarchy of the bureaucratic structures that run the economy, the enterprises report to general directorates, central administrations, branch ministries, planning organisms, and all the other offices and ministries at the related levels (Labor Ministry, Finance Ministry, Central Bank, Ministry for Science and Technology, State Committee for Price Control, Committees for Material-Technical Resources and Supply, Central Statistical Administration, and so forth)—a bureaucratic apparatus of unbelievable dimensions. There are in Moscow, in addition to the political ministries customary in Western countries, another 41 economic ministries, each employing several thousands of officials. The same situation is repeated in all the republics of the Soviet Union with corresponding branches at the regional level. Such a gigantic state apparatus for the planning and control of the even greater apparatus of enterprises and enterprise associations exists in each of the Eastern European countries. This represents a concentration of such bureaucratic nonsense and unrealistic formalism that the losses to society incurred by the costs alone are multiplied by their varied activities. Unfortunately, there are no statistics to disclose these losses.

It is even impossible to know the exact number of bureaucrats since this is one of the best-kept secrets of the bureaucratic system itself that must not be revealed to the working class, the "ruling class." Only the bureaucracy of the Communist Party apparatus that controls the economic and state bureaucracies is informed on the extent and activities of subordinated bureaucratic administrations. But the party bureaucracy is the one which knows best that its existence depends on the whole system and that it therefore cannot afford to uncover the engrained bureaucratic characteristics of this system. This explains why the system itself is not described as "bureaucratic" and that instead its bureaucratic shortcomings are periodically criticized by the party leaders. It is the party bureaucracy itself that starts criticizing the state and economic apparatuses as soon as the economic situation gets out of hand and threatens to

TABLE 1: Effectivity of Administrative Organizations

	Number of Enterprises	Number of Employed in Production	Production per Employed	Gross Industrial Product	Cost of Central Administrative Apparatus
Ministries at Union Level for:					
Heavy machinery and transport vehicle building	99.2	104.3	111.6	116.7	128.0
Electrical engineering	94.8	108.5	111.5	118.0	135.5
Chemical and petrochemical machinery	103.5	107.1	117.0	125.0	142.0
Machine-building for construction industry	102.8	105.1	117.9	124.8	126.8
Agricultural machinery	107.1	104.5	112.7	117.9	131.0
Ministries at Republic Level for:					
Metal-working industry	101.8	105.2	110.0	115.5	133.0
Coal mining	97.0	98.0	106.8	104.9	123.3
Oil production	97.5	104.4	108.5	113.9	120.6

Source: J. Kusnezow and A. Tichomirova, "Effectivity of Administrative Organizations in Industrial Sectors," Voprosy Ekonomiky, no. 11 (1970):76.

arouse discontent in the population, particularly in the working class. At such times there is growing criticism of the bureucratism in the ministries, in the central administrations, or in the enterprises. However, no mention is ever made of the fact that the central apparatus is not at all capable of recognizing the intricate economic complexities in view of the millions of ever-changing lines of products, not to mention of respecting and harmonizing by systematic control the whole range of economic activities throughout the country.

The basic problem of the insolvable conflict between aggregation and disaggregation of production information is overlooked. From the enterprises to the center, information on the quantity of required goods is being aggregated in big general categories of products. Therefore, the central planning office does not know how much of one or the other product is actually in demand but only balances the highly aggregated input-output relations. Except for a few categories, the goals of the plan are aggregated and communicated to the enterprises via the lines of authority within the hierarchical apparatus. At the enterprise level they are disaggregated and transformed into concrete production decisions and activities. There is a refusal to understand that essential contradictions between the general, centrally planned production decisions on the one hand and the actual individual decisions at the enterprise management level on the other hand do not only, and not substantially, result from the fact that such enormous amounts of concrete goods cannot be systematically planned, not even with the help of the most modern computer systems. The major reason has to be seen in the conflict between the interests of the enterprise collective and those of the central agencies.

While the essential task of the central planning and control organisms is to maximize the output of the enterprise in relation to the input or, in other words, to minimize their input as compared to a given output, the enterprise management will always be intent on building up reserves for an easier fulfillment of their planning indicators. It will be in their interest to obtain a maximum input as compared to the demanded output, or to achieve a minimum output in relation to the obtainable input. This basic contradiction constitutes the major problem of a centrally planned economy; it cannot be overcome by any partial reform, change of indicators or incentives, and certainly not by administrative reorganization.

Equally, the idea of eliminating the shortcomings of a bureaucratic administration with the help of modern optimal economic calculations by using extensive computer systems to arrive at a more efficient planning, ignores the fact that a central planning agency cannot optimize the *microstructure* of production involving hundreds of thousands of different products. It can only make calculations for highly aggregated categories of products and/or a few concrete preferential products. In a situation of nonexisting market interests and lack of competition, a possible practical application of such optimal calculations for highly aggregated groups of products would not eliminate the basic problem of a centrally planned economy, namely, the *disinterest* on the part of the branch organs and of the enterprises to try to achieve an optimally effective production development and to provide the central planning organisms with the necessary information. Equally, they would not be interested in transforming global plan targets as fixed by the central administration into concrete production decisions most likely to reach a societal optimum. This kind of *disinterest* is the basic problem in industrial and possibly even more so in agricultural enterprises. And this kind of disinterest is impossible to overcome with incentives offered by the central agencies.

The enterprises will always attempt to have the central planning agencies fix as low a performance target as possible in relation to existent labor and capital, whether the planned and demanded output is defined by planning indicators for gross production, net production, profit, or productivity, or whether the production is controlled by a smaller or larger number of indicators. Also, enterprise managers will always be interested in supplying the central planning agencies with information geared to favorably influence decisions on reserves and on conditions for the fulfillment of plans. This cannot be changed by any kind of incentives since the central organs lack concrete knowledge of the production potentials in the enterprises and thus have to rely on their information. Therefore, even if the planning organs would tie bonuses to the fulfillment of the productivity growth rate, of the production cost decrease, and so forth, the enterprises will always have a strong interest in transmitting false data in order to be allocated relatively low planning targets that are easy to fulfill and entitle them to higher bonuses, wage increases, and other benefits.

The centrally determined remunerations—in the largest sense— of the enterprises computed on the basis of their own data constitute an inherent contradiction of this planning system. Since material reward remains the most powerful incentive for overtime, additional effort, and productivity increase, and since the central organs that decide on these incentives never receive concrete data from the enterprise management, the basic information bias will never be eliminated. Purely moral incentives and nonmaterial rewards would not only result in developing insufficient achievement and efficiency in the enterprises but would, in addition, again be based on biased data coming from below.

Those who simply refuse to recognize this built-in contradiction of the system or who try to cover it up with slogans of "socialist consciousness development" are either hypocrites motivated by their own attractive positions within the system or they are pursuing idealistic pipe dreams. In the latter case, the reason is a misunderstanding about the fact that the majority of the population for a long time in the future cannot possibly be interested in their mostly exhausting and monotonous work as such but will work for remuneration and consumption only. Evidently this will result in bargaining for a minimum increase in productivity (qualitative production changes, too, can be considered a performance) at maximum wages. Lenin had to experience this very soon after the revolution, just as the Czech, Hungarian, Polish, and other communist politicians found out after a few years of revolutionary enthusiasm. The Cuban party leadership was forced to admit to this fact after the years of unsuccessful Guevara dreams and the Chinese eventually had the same experience.

From time to time, Marxist-oriented theories are discussed that basically disapprove of Soviet bureaucratism and even deny that the Soviet system has any truly socialist characteristics, but that at the same time refuse with indignation any attempts at introducing socialist market relations into the system. Referring to the positive results of the economic development in China, A. Carlo[31] blames the existence of bureaucratic rule for the Soviet economic difficulties. In contrast to the Chinese system, bureaucracy in the Soviet Union results in a planned control of the economy to such an extent that it is no longer in the interest of the working classes and in fact leads to their exploitation and estrangement. Carlo's criticism can be accepted as being justified thus far; he then goes on to explain in more detail the mechanism of bureaucratic rule in the Soviet Union and its consequences. However, Carlo's negative attitude toward reforms that aim at introducing elements of a market economy in Eastern Europe and his rejection of socialist market relations[32] are based on a basic underestimation of the material interest on the part of the workers and other toilers at the present stage of development of labor and its decisive character. Basically, Carlo assumed that it would be sufficient to replace a bureaucratic rule with a "real worker democracy."[33] According to Carlo, the existence of such a proletarian democracy would mean that, "The working class would have to make all the essential decisions necessary for the well-being of the community in a general and free discussion, and thus set a framework in the form of a plan. The management of the individual enterprises would have to participate in this process of clarification and decisions, not on a competitive basis but in cooperation with the workers. The goal of the production organized in this fashion would be to produce consumer goods such as required by society. This model would be a genuinely socialist one."[34]

First, Carlo greatly simplifies the origins of Soviet bureaucracy, which he describes as the result of the "weakening of the proletariat during the war and the civil war, the elimination of its avant-garde, the impossibility of reconstructing a new political worker's avant-garde, and of the necessity of having to resort to the personnel of the former czarist state apparatus."[35] Second, he believes that the conscience and ethics of genuine workers and their avant-garde would be sufficient to guarantee a production development geared to satisfy requirements and the need for maximum efficiency. This theory simplifies the problem of optimal production development in a highly industrialized country to a point where it can only be considered the outcome of purely idealistic and wishful thinking.

This kind of reasoning is based on the assumption that enterprises managed by workers' councils would be able to always correctly *project*—without the help of a market—the type of goods to produce in order to satisfy the needs of consumers throughout the country. However, Carlo does not explain how this procedure could actually be put in practice in view of the millions of different types of goods to produce (as he himself points out) and of the constantly changing structure in demands. How would an enterprise be able to react to an increase in demand if an increase in its production was dependent on an increase in supplies of products by hundreds of different suppliers, subcontractors, and so forth, that is, dependent on the proportionally increasing production of raw materials, semi-finished goods, equipment, energy, and so forth? He does not answer this question. It would necessitate either an ex post facto adjustment of the production as in a market system but without the demand and supply of stabilizing prices (which involves numerous supply shortages and unfulfilled requirements). Or, one would have to try to plan ex ante the entire production including all its multifaceted complexities and a concrete projection of economic requirements. As Carlo himself admits,[36] this would be beyond the capabilities of workers' representatives as well as of a bureaucratic planning agency.

The idea has been put forward that it would be sufficient to plan only the *global* production development centrally, that is, only the sectorial structure according to *global* studies of requirements, and to leave it to the enterprises to determine the actual microstructure of production. However, this concept neglects the decisive relationship between centrally established capital growth rates (for individual sectors) and actual production capacities of the enterprises. Just as it is the case today, any error in the central investment planning would result in production developments that do not correspond to the requirements (and that, once more, results in shortages). On the other hand, Carlo assumes that all enterprise collectives are interested in being flexible by changing the microstructure of their production according to changes in actual requirements, by improving their product quality and by introducing new and more useful goods (the most essential condition for technical progress), by making optimal economic use of given production factors and arriving at a production increase with the help of improved technology, production organization, and division of labor. All this is without corresponding increase in their incomes—just for the sake of "socialist morality." Here we have definite proof of the fact that he underestimates material motivations for additional labor in socialism, a fact that even Marx and Lenin have stressed as being typical of this stage in socialist development.

As for the conditions of production demanded by Carlo, all structural changes, quality improvements, product innovations, technological progress, and so forth would have to be rewarded as additional work performance because, at the present stage of development of productive forces, work for most people is a heavy burden, it does not represent their own immediate interests, and it is supplied mainly as a condition for consumption. If collectives that take advantage of all the possibilities of optimal production development through higher work performance would not receive higher remunerations than collectives that make only limited efforts without using all their potential, the former would very soon slow down their efforts. But because all these entirely different and constantly changing possibilities for improving production cannot be planned, measured, and evaluated by any superior organ, and because only a real market mechanism with its price movement, competition, and market-related income can motivate the enterprises to keep trying for optimal production, even in a system such as conceived by Carlo (for highly industrialized countries)[37] production efficiency would lag far behind that of the capitalist system. In the final analysis the consequences as far as the population is concerned should be very similar to those in the Soviet bureaucratic system.

One of the essential aspects of the progress made by Czech theoreticians was to recognize the *specific conflicts of interests* that are inevitable in socialist production systems because of permanent systemic *conditions of labor and consumption*. These contradictions cannot be solved by centralized planning and control (and even less by moral appeals) but only by means of a socialist, *regulated* market in the framework of *macroeconomic planning*. Those, who like Carlo, neglect to recognize this *problem of conflicting interests* and even pretend that the Czech reform movement has not provided any new theoretical insights [38] actually fall back to the theoretical stage typical of the Leninist era, which was characterized by an incredibly simplified concept of economic interests.

Neither Lenin nor his successors were able to admit to anything more than that material incentives do exist also in socialism and should be taken advantage of. However, Lenin had not understood that entire enterprise collectives and their administrations also should be rewarded according to their work performance and their production of commodities that have utility value for society, and that the reward cannot be guaranteed without market prices and competition. Similarly, the highest representatives of the party apparatus today cannot, and *do not want* to, understand this situation for if they did they would negate the necessary existence of their most reliable support, namely, the extended bureaucratic state apparatus and its supremacy.

Only bureaucrats can believe in the possibility of inducing enterprise associations and their management into optimal productivity by means of moral appeals. Formalized bureaucratic thinking lacks any genuine understanding of morality, its nature, origin, and influence,[39] as well as of the nature of the conflict existing between societal interests on the one hand, and economically determined interests of the enterprises on the other hand. This is amply proven by the increasing number of moralizing treatises written by systemic ideologists in view of providing the bureaucracy with convenient excuses.[41]

The inability and the refusal to disclose the real causes of an inefficient and socially harmful production process is also demonstrated by the fact that all economic shortcomings are consistently blamed on the "insufficient socialist morals" of the working individuals, as if "different morals" would, first, make the enterprises acquire the ability of knowing which are the *optimal* production methods and production lines and, second, ensure a production activity at the enterprise level that would amount to being directed against the economic interest of these enterprise collectives. What a typically bureaucratic attitude: to complain about the "insufficient socialist morals" of the people without a single one of the bureaucrats being able to say what the optimal production of one enterprise should look like, and without understanding that such maximum output is even being curtailed by the central plan and its dictates. Only market-oriented enterprises (and this equally applies to collectively owned enterprises) have to aim for maximum output in relation to their input, for appropriate production structures, and, in general, for optimal production and marketing results if they want to compare favorably with the competition and turn the advantage of free-market pricing into maximum profits. Wage increases and bonus allocations cannot be obtained by means of biased data passed on to superiors, nor by individual quantitative production increases and fictitious plan fulfillment arrived at by structural changes. It can only be achieved by a real increase in efficiency. But as long as these features of socialist market conditions are not accepted by the communist power bureaucracy, society will have to cope with the conflict of interests between bureaucratic organisms and the economic base, as well as with the resulting information bias, red tape, and increasing economic losses. Whenever complaints and criticism within the party apparatus start increasing, when the population becomes restless and the party leadership insecure because of supply shortages, interrupted production, unwanted products, declining quality, unfinished investment projects, rising costs, and declining productivity, the party apparatus at that moment judges it time to criticize bureaucratism in the state apparatus. However, nobody can actually be found guilty, nor can any causes inherent in the system be pointed to; instead, a reorganization of the administrative apparatus is announced as the solution to all problems.

It would be a special subject of research to make a list of all the reorganizations of the administrative apparatus that have so far taken place in the communist countries. Ministries of different sectors were first grouped together and then separated a few years later; new ministries were created to be eliminated shortly afterward; trust organizations were transformed into ministerial central administrations and later changed back into general directorates; centralization was followed by decentralization until centralization was restored; enterprises were integrated in enterprise associations and a few years later became independent again; the position of the ministries was first strengthened, then weakened, only to be strengthened again a few years later, and so forth. The following is a typical example. The CSSR on January 1, 1953, adopted the Soviet government system, and the number of ministries increased considerably. General directorates were abolished and replaced by central administrations incorporated in the ministries. Decision making at the enterprise level was limited, especially in Slovakia since the central administrations had their headquarters in Prague. In 1958-59, the central administrations were abolished and replaced by production enterprise associations (VHJ) with a common directorate (an institution similar to the former general directorates). In 1962,

Novotny blamed the VHJ for considerable economic failures and curtailed their independence from the ministries. The powerful position of the economic ministries was again reduced in 1965 while enterprise associations in the form of trusts or concerns were created. In 1972 the ministries' position was once more strengthened and a differentiated three-tier control system established: ministry-trust or branch enterprise organ-enterprises.

When Khrushchev in 1957 engineered the replacement of the traditional system of economic ministries with a system of regional economic councils he neglected one "small detail": to abolish central planning and to introduce market-economy structures. The central Gosplan was to continue planning the entire Soviet economy and regulating input-output relations among all the economic sectors of the country. As it turned out, the ministries were missing as the necessary link to the enterprises of the different sectors. Instead, the Gosplan had to cooperate with a great number of branch administrations within the regional economic councils in order to be able to coordinate communication among the different sectors throughout the country. The Gosplan managed to accomplish this Sisyphean undertaking only by means of a considerable expansion of its own branch administrations, which steadily grew into small branch ministries. When he saw that the ministerial bureaucracy that he had chased from Moscow was coming back to establish itself in a new organization, an angry Khrushchev turned to decentralizing the Gosplan as well. When on top of this he started to divide the party apparatus into a special industrial and a specifically agricultural apparatus, he became too dangerous not only to the state bureaucracy but also to the party bureaucracy. He had to be removed from power. Thus it became possible, with the support of the decisive bureaucratic power, for Breshnev as representative of the party apparatus and for Kosygin as representative of the planning bureaucracy to be chosen as Khrushchev's successors.

Brezhnev later justified the reintroduction of industrial branch ministries in Moscow by saying: "In the course of the past few years certain negative features have begun to appear, such as a slowing-down in production and labor growth rates, decreased effectiveness of production funds and investment. Without a critical stand . . . our progress will be rather unsatisfactory. . . . In order to improve the administration of the industrial sectors and to accelerate scientific-technological progress, ministries will be created at the Union and Republic levels. They will be responsible for their specific sectors, for a high technical standard of production, and for meeting the country's needs in industrial commodities. . . ."[41]

Thus, at the time, ministries were being reintroduced in view of promoting labor productivity and efficiency. Although the criticism has remained the same, it now serves to justify another decentralization process: the introduction of *industrial* associations (of large enterprises). Again, they are to take over certain functions and some authority from the ministries in the hope of accelerating *technological* progress and of increasing efficiency.

However, the ministries cannot be abolished, for in a central planning system they are the indispensable intermediaries in the line of command to the different economic sectors. They have to decide on the activities of all enterprises and factories of a specific production sector, and without their decisions it is impossible to coordinate the activities in the different branches. Only when enterprises from different sectors are linked and coordinated by a market is there no need for *branch ministries* to take the role of coordinators. But it is exactly this very important function of coordinating by the branch ministries that is being curtailed by bureaucratic sectoral interests within certain ministries. Such interests interfere with actual branch coordination in the same way that bureaucrats of a certain administration (which includes ministries) develop specific group interests (which we will call sectoral interests). This is demonstrated in the fact that their own formal performance (which determines promotions, salary raises, and so forth) has priority over the achievements of other sectors and ministries.

The methods applied to achieve plan fulfillment within the sector for which the ministry is responsible can become less important than the plan fulfillment. In simplified terms, each ministry struggles for priority allocations of capital, raw material, and work force for its own branch even at the expense of other branches because this facilitates its own plan fulfillment. As long as the plan is formally fulfilled, each ministry is inclined to overlook certain inaccuracies occuring in the process of plan fulfillment on the part of subordinated enterprises (even in the form of structural manipulations or price rises). If it benefits plan fulfillment, each ministry will approve qualitative product deterioration in the subordinated enterprises and cover up for insufficient innovation—all the while accusing other enterprises in other branches of having deteriorated in quality. Such modes of behavior are relatively frequent because both the bureaucracy and its highest representative, the minister, are primarily interested in their own achievement and success.

Naturally, egotistical sectoral interests are the greatest enemy of any coordination effort. Instead of achieving a harmonization of objectively related and mutually dependent activities of enterprises belonging to all economic sectors, these activities are even more disrupted and made to contradict each other. While the market, by considerations of profits or losses, pressures the enterprises into respecting the buyers' interests to the greatest possible extent, the "conscious" coordination of supplier-buyer relations is leading to such contradictions in this relationship as have rarely existed before. Although the sectoral interests as well as the sectoral behavior are persistently being criticized and attempts are made time and again to remove this shortcoming by means of reorganizations, the specific interests of this bureaucracy cannot be changed or eliminated, in the same way that a system of central planning cannot function without the controlling and deciding actions of bureaucrats. The sectoral interests are only one of many other concrete manifestations of these bureaucratic interests. Given the best of wills, the desperate organizational changes and repeated reorganizations cannot replace one element, namely the economic initiative—stimulated by market price mechanism and competitive pressure—which is so typical of enterprises operating in a market economy.

However, the party bureaucracy cannot afford to allow a change in the established system, for a change would amount to granting the enterprises real independence and to eliminating central tutelage and control. The powerful position of the entire party apparatus would be undermined if enterprise activity and management were no longer determined and controlled by supraenterprise organisms and indirectly, as we shall see, by the party bureaucracy itself. This is the reason why all the ideas and movements of reform recurrent throughout the history of the Soviet system have been suppressed and condemned. Those among the reformers who have recognized the uniqueness and necessity of market relations even among socialist enterprises and who more or less consistently advocated the application of their concepts have been most strongly attacked by the party bureaucracy as "counterrevolutionaries" and eventually silenced.[42]

The very fact that there has never been any reaction in the official party press to all the factual argumentation presented or published by reformers in the USSR, in Poland, Hungary, the CSSR, and so forth, but that the party bureaucracy always contented itself with labeling these efforts "bourgeois treason," "return to capitalism," "petty bourgeois revisionism" is clear enough proof of bureaucratic power interests. The party organs have not once dared to analyze the reasons why the structure of production remains in constant contradiction with the structure of requirements (of demand). Instead of carrying out such analysis, two alleged causes have been advanced for 50 years now to explain the situation: the "insufficient socialist morals of enterprise management" and "insufficient control of production by the party." The remedy is believed to come from repeated appeals to enterprise management and to the working masses.

The important questions are: Why did the party bureaucracy succeed in suppressing for so long society's experience and rational understanding? How did it manage to maintain for decades an absolute bureaucratic system, neglecting the real interests of the majority of the people and ruling the country from the removed position of a power elite? These very questions are at the same time questions about the mechanism of power in communist systems.

NOTES

1. Ota Šik, *The Third Way—Marxist-Leninist Theory and Modern Industrial Society*, (London-New York, 1976).

2. See also Marx's letter to L. Kugelmann, April 17, 1871.

3. A. Carlo, *Politische und Oekonomische Struktur der USSR (1917-1975)* [Political and economic structure of the USSR] (Berlin, 1972), p. 21.

4. L. Trotsky, *Stalin*.

5. Ibid.

6. This can not, and should not, be interpreted as an evaluation or even condemnation of the "cultural revolution," which would be impossible to do on the basis of the presently available, limited information. I want to point out, however, that this specific development process, too, did not result in the elimination of conditions that I believe to be the real cause of the specific socialist bureaucratization process.

7. More on this subject in K. Marx, *The Eighteenth Brumaire of Louis Bonaparte* and I. Deutscher, *Marxism and the USSR*.

8. The following sources are particularly relevant here: K. Marx, *The Eighteenth Brumaire of Louis Bonaparte*; ibid., *Critique of Hegel's Philosophy of Right*; M. Weber, *Economy and Society*; P. J. Proudhon, *Confessions of a Revolutionary*; M. Bakunin, *Philosophy of Action*; N. Luhmann, *Theory of Administrative Science*; R. Merton, "Bureaucratic Structure and Personality," in *Buerokratische Organisation* [Bureaucratic organization], ed. R. Mayntz (Cologne, 1968); R. Dahrendorf, *Konflikt und Freiheit* (Munich, 1972); and W. D. Narr and A. Offe, eds., *Wohlfahrtsstaat und Massenloyalitaet* (Cologne, 1975).

9. Weber, *Economy and Society*; R. Mayntz, ed., *Buerokratische Organisation*, [Bureaucratic organization] (Cologne, 1968).

10. Weber, ibid.

11. Ibid.

12. See *Encyclopedia Britannica*, 4:420, for the definitions of "bureaucrat" and "bureaucracy."

13. Weber, ibid.

14. F. Engels, *The Origins of Family, Private Property, and State*.

15. Weber, ibid.

16. See R. Merton, "Bureaucratic Structure and Personality."

17. Ota Šik, *Oekonomie, Interessen, Politik* [Economy, interests, and politics] (Berlin, 1966), p. 490.

18. C. N. Parkinson, *Parkinson's Law or The Pursuit of Progress* (London, 1965), p. 12.

19. K. Marx, *Critique of Hegel's Philosophy of Right.*

20. R. Merton, "Bureaucratic Structure and Personality."

21. Marx, ibid.

22. Ibid.

23. Weber, ibid.

24. Marx, ibid.

25. A. Pelinka, *Dynamische Demokratie* [Dynamic democracy] (Stuttgart, 1974), p. 19.

26. Weber, ibid.

27. Ibid.

28. Ibid.

29. W. Leonard, *Am Vorabend einer neuen Revolution?* [On the eve of a new revolution?] (Munich, 1975), p. 106.

30. For more on this subject see Šik, *The Third Way*, chaps. 4, 5, and 6.

31. Carlo, ibid., p. 63.

32. Ibid., p. 80.

33. Ibid., p. 69.

34. Ibid. p. 84.

35. Ibid., p. 60.

36. Ibid., p. 67.

37. See also Šik, ibid., chap. 3.

38. Carlo, ibid. Carlo knows so little about the Czech theoretical development that he even identifies it with Liberman's theory (p. 80), and asserts that, compared to the Polish development of the 1950s, it did not make any essential contributions,

39. More on this subject in Šik, ibid., chap. 9.

40. A typical example is the essay by M. Randova, "Origin and Development of Socialist Morals," in *Rude Pravo*, July 17, 1975.

41. L. Brezhnev, *Following Lenin—Speeches and Essays.*

42. Opposition comes mostly from noneconomists who do not understand the market mechanism at all and oppose this concept for the simple reason that they identify market with capitalism. A typical example is the nonsensical comments of the journalist J. Hajek, chief editor of the party organ *Tvorba* in the CSSR, in his book *Demokratisierung oder Demontage* [Democratization or dismantling?] (Munich, 1969).

3
MECHANISM OF THE COMMUNIST POWER SYSTEM

THE LEADING ROLE OF THE PARTY

In all the countries within the Soviet sphere of influence the "leading" role of the Communist Party is understood to mean that the organs and the apparatus of the Communist Party determine all public activities, all aspects of societal life, organisms, institutions, enterprises, and associations. By incorporating the leading role of the Communist Party into the constitutions of most of these countries, a political party has been officially transformed into a supreme state institution that can rightfully claim the administration and control of all aspects of public life.[1] In effect, the reality of the party's powerful position has been legalized. But it also implies that because of this legalization any opposition to the party can be interpreted as subversive activity.

A leadership role as defined in these terms according to which the party is not only leading in establishing essential political and economic development goals but practically controls the entire range of a society's activities can not be assumed by ordinary communists and their assemblies but can only be accomplished by a highly organized bureaucracy. Such a task requires a hierarchically structured apparatus consisting of secretariats in all large enterprises, of district and county secretariats, regional secretariats, and the central secretariat of the entire federation as the most powerful domain of this bureaucratic organization. The functionaries employed in these secretariats number in the thousands or even tens of thousands depending on the size of the country. All leading cadres of these secretariats are selected, appointed, and controlled by a superior agency. District secretaries select the secretaries in the enterprises and are themselves appointed by the county secretaries who in turn are nominated by the central secretaries.

For all the important sectors of a country's activities (economy, defense and security, law, education and culture, medicine and social sciences, sports, propaganda and agitation, information media, mass organizations, and so forth), the party apparatus has special divisions under a head of department with several of these divisions reporting to a secretary. The First Secretary, sometimes called General Secretary, is responsible not only for the entire secretariat but also for particularly important divisions as, for example, the department of party organization, of defense and security, and so forth. It is the task of these divisions to control the activities of all dependent institutions, to keep in permanent contact with their leading cadres, to write reports on their activities, to get to know their collaborators and to recruit new cadres, to submit an occasional analysis in order to discover problems, difficulties, or maybe new developmental factors, to establish, if necessary, proposals for change, and so forth. The division heads in the Central Secretariat wield more power than the official state ministers, for the latter have to obtain the division heads' approval for all important measures and actions.

The secretaries make up the collective control organ headed by the First Secretary (in the central administration as well as at the district and county levels). Even though all secretariats are subordinate to "elected" party organs, this does not really have much meaning. Officially, the highest party organ is the Party Congress: it is responsible for establishing the general line of party politics and for electing the Central Committee and the Central Control Commission. From the ranks of the Central Committee are then chosen the members of the Politburo (Party Chairman, Executive, Presidium),[2] whose head assumes at the same time the function of First Secretary. The Politburo is responsible for the party's activities during intervals between the sessions of the Central Committee (about once every three months), for establishing reports, and for implementing its decisions. Membership, varying between 10 and 20, is reserved for the most powerful among the party functionaries who are each backed by a reliable apparatus (party, ministries, military, state security, unions, and so forth), in other words, by the highest representatives of the bureaucracy. But even here the party apparatus has secured its decisive influence, as we shall see below. In reality, elections and votes play a very minor role, for the actual policies and decisions are shaped and taken by the party apparatus and the party secretaries.

During the years before Stalin seized power or, rather, eliminated all dangerous opponents, the sessions of the Central Committee and of the party congresses were characterized by genuine discussions and votes. Since then, the party has been brought into line, a development that today is still going on in all the countries within the Soviet sphere of influence, and which is one of the most typical characteristics of Stalinization. With a few exceptions, such as when the First Secretary is removed from his position by insurgent secretaries and members of the Politburo (which is what happened to Khrushchev), there is no genuine opposition in the sessions of the Central Committee and at the party congresses. Discussions relating to proposals and discussions that have all been prepared by the secretaries and are mostly submitted by the First Secretary are generally of a purely rhetorical nature. The only results are relatively unimportant additions or amendments; there are never any real counterproposals. Almost invariably the original plans are unanimously accepted by acclamation. This procedure cannot be explained by the fact that the bureaucratic apparatus only submits perfect proposals and that there is no need for counterproposals corresponding even better to the people's interests. The real reason is the total dependency on the party apparatus of all members of the "elected" party organs, as well as their reluctance to be in opposition since the consequences of past attempts have long since become a warning experience for all party members.

The methods applied by the party apparatus and by the secretaries as the most powerful representatives to dominate all party members, all extraparty institutions and organs, and, therefore, the entire population can basically be summarized in three categories: cadre politics, system of repression and corruption, and ideological monopoly.

CADRE POLITICS

Once the party apparatus has been set up, it develops an organized system of self-reproduction. New members have to conform to the established pattern of interests and must have the required ideological background. Although personal career ambitions and power interests are part of the general personality makeup of a party bureaucrat, the rules of the game demand that these features remain undisclosed. The appearance given is one of complete dedication to the idea and to the goal. Requirements as expressed by hierarchical superiors are ostentatiously respected at all times. However, the apparatus' activities are determined by bureaucratic regulations. The best conditions for a functionary's career are not independent and critical thinking and understanding for the people's dissatisfaction and complaints but the ability to approve all party directives as well as the willingness to publicly defend these directives at all times. In addition, a functionary must have a feel for the prevailing political "current" and support the "right" upcoming man in the higher rank. It is also important to be able to stress one's own "modesty" and "unselfishness," to demonstrate reliability, and to inform superiors on words and actions of their personal enemies. These will always be the most reliable characteristics and attitudes for a party functionary who is intent on rapid promotion.

Every selection of a cadre, his initial acceptance into the party apparatus, any successive promotions, and, eventually, his election to the most important positions are acts that always have to be initiated, suggested, and decided by a higher functionary, such as department head, secretary, or Politburo member. However, since every functionary has his own career in mind, the selection and promotion of cadres—cadre politics—is the most decisive means of promoting one's own career opportunities. The greater the number of reliable, personally dedicated, and influential cadres a functionary manages to place in important positions, the greater will be his own political power and influence. This is the reason why cadre politics is not only the decisive means for the qualitative reproduction of the entire party apparatus as the real power elite, but is at the same time the most essential instrument in the permanent struggle for personal power among the party functionaries.

Although the bureaucratic party apparatus may appear to be very united to the masses "which lack socialist consciousness," the infighting among its "professional revolutionaries" is considerable. The problem is not only political career thinking and opportunism as they are typical of any political party, but a real power struggle fought with the same ruthlessness and brutality as the ideologically motivated "intensified class war." All the in-party spying and allegations of "wrong" thinking and uncommunist behavior in other people, all the accusing reports and intrigues, the way of getting rid of personal enemies and of staging show trials to liquidate former leading personalities, the quiet "elimination" of all too popular men whose official trial would have been politically risky—in a totalitarian system, these and similar practices take on dimensions inconceivable in a democracy.

The relationships existing between the functionaries in the highest party organs are not easy to describe. Mutual distrust and fear, allegations, tension, hypocrisy, and surveillance are so intense that for these functionaries total alienation becomes a condition of life. These people feel constantly threatened and afraid of being labeled political deviationists, a threat which they try to fight off by asserting their power over others. "Try to deflect accusations of your own deviations by providing proof of other people's deviating behavior—this is the only way to stay on the winning side." This permanent covert fight for power, the concealment of one's personal opinion in order not to become a minority, the importance of being among the first to discover in time the aspirations of one or the other of the leaders, these are the elements creating an environment where only the most unscrupulous and reckless among the bureaucrats can manage to survive and to advance. But he has to be an expert in cadre politics. How did a man like Novotny, who was a completely uneducated person incapable of giving even the shortest intelligent speech without a paper, manage to remain for so many years at the head of the Czechoslovakian Communist Party and government?[3] The answer is that he mastered to perfection the art of cadre politics.

The selection of future cadres starts in the party's base organizations, or even at the level of the communist youth organizations. Each district secretary employs a great number of activists in addition to his own collaborators so that he can closely follow the activities at the base, observing discussions and members' attitudes in order to have detailed knowledge of all cadres. This information is computed and constantly updated in special files. Particularly important is the data on a member's political "reliability," his conformism, and active participation, although these general characteristics are not as essential for a political career as those mentioned above that have to come to the division head's or secretary's personal attention.

Ordinarily, those who show the qualities of a future functionary are sent to a special party school to acquire the necessary ideological knowledge and background and to make proof once more of their special mentality. There are monthly district schools as well as centrally organized training courses. The highest educational level is provided by the four-year party colleges, with standard graduation and the additional possibility of acquiring the title of "candidate of political sciences" after presentation of a thesis. Future members of the central party apparatus are recruited primarily among these party school graduates and political science majors; similarly, they are found in all the central organs of other mass organizations as well as in all major sectors of activity, such as unions, youth organizations, state bureaucracy, military, police, newspaper administration, business, and so forth.

Cadre politics as well as promotion of party bureaucracy interests have to be covered up and must not interfere with democratic appearances. The party therefore tries to maintain the illusion of decision making by elected organs, but neither the ordinary party members nor the mass of nonparty citizens believe in this myth anymore. The fact that "democratic" elections nevertheless are still being enacted is one of the many bureaucratic absurdities of the system.

The preparation and manipulation of "pseudodemocratic" decisions is one of the major functions of the party apparatus. On the basis of the cadre files and with the help of all available activists, the elections to the committees of the base organizations, the district, and county conferences and especially the party congresses have to be prepared as to cadre attendance and subject matter. It is essential that the "most reliable," most eager, and most disciplined among the cadres be delegated to attend conferences and party congresses. At the very start, the process of voting in the base organizations for delegates to the district conferences selected and proposed by the county secretariat is normally carried out by simple hand raising and without counterproposals. The reason is not only the fear of ordinary members of being singled out as oppositionalists but also their incapacity as individuals to counter the carefully prepared proposals of superior cadres or, in other words, the impossiblity of submitting well-conceived counterproposals since the slightest indication of forming groups is suppressed as "fractionalization."

Although the base organizations are constantly urged to be active, they cannot afford to express "wrong" opinions and to oppose the "party line." The Central Committee has never hesitated to exclude an entire organization that dared express oppositional views. The indifference and passivity of the majority of ordinary party members finds an easy explanation in their awareness that public opinion and election processes are strictly shaped and channeled by the party apparatus.

This mechanism and the selection of basically conforming delegates to the party congress create an environment that eliminates the danger of having to deal with oppositional or independent delegates, not to mention entire groups. The mechanism functions also in parties that are not yet in power but have a well-organized apparatus. The established party leadership or central party apparatus prepares the drafts for all decisions, resolutions, and candidates' lists for the election of new organs on the basis of carefully considered cadre selections with the goal of securing a totally compliant new central committee. Even the discussions held at the party congress are carefully prepared and staged by the district secretariats and delegations under the responsibility of the First District Secretary. Due to the overwhelming number of prepared contributions to the debates and of formal speeches by foreign guests and official speakers there is no danger of someone interfering with the discussions and disturbing the solemn and bureaucratically staged event.

In any case, no contribution to the debate could possibly have any real political impact. An individual who is denied the right to unite with his like-minded friends will invariably fail in trying to fight the opinions of this most powerful and well-organized apparatus. The previously determined and limited duration of the party congresses, their solemn staging, and the fact that each act is controlled from the bureaucratic wings make these events a demonstration of pure formality. The lists of the predestined candidates for all "elections" cannot even be checked by the delegates, not to mention the fact that it is impossible to set up countercandidates on the basis of organized agreements. In reality, therefore, the party congresses do not decide on the programs and political platforms but uncritically approve whatever the party apparatus and the outgoing Politburo have prepared. Also, the party congress does not *elect* the incoming central committee but passively accepts those candidates who conform to the apparatus' interests and therefore are liable to warrant the continuity of the existing power system. We have here the well-functioning mechanism of the continuous reproduction of a system-preserving power elite, a mechanism that allows for an occasional turnover among the members of this elite but only as a result of a personal power struggle within the party leadership, and not under the influence of the mass of party members.

Logically, the same system of preparation, selection, and nomination of cadres by the party apparatus is applied when it comes to filling the key positions of power and control in the state administration, in the economic sector, and in all other spheres of influence. There are cadre nomenclatures with detailed instructions as to which positions are to be filled by what party organs, which functions are under the responsibility of the Central Committee, of the Politburo, the Secretariat, the secretariat divisions, the county and district committees, or their secretariats.[4]

But even the cadre nominations that are officially approved by the Central Committee and not by the Secretariat are determined de facto by the apparatus since the vote by hand raising taken by the Central Committee is no more than a formality. Although the mem-

bers of the Politburo themselves may submit various cadre nominations given the fact that cadre politics is one of the essential tools in
the covert power struggle among the prospective candidates for the
position of First Secretary, the most important and active role is
played by the central apparatus, which has the most complete and
up-to-date information on all the cadres. This means that the secretaries, and above all the First Secretary, have a distinct advantage
over the other members of the Politburo. However, sometimes the
other members, too, manage to promote "their" people with the help
of their own apparatus, on the basis of better information, or by
means of clever tactics.

Since cadre politics is one of the essential instruments of power,
the members of the Politburo are particularly attentive to this kind
of political activity. Each one of them has to carefully hide his
personal power interests behind the "concern for socialist interests."
In reality, though, the greatest and most useful political skill in the
permanent power struggle is the ability to promote those cadres who
are dedicated to their promoters but not brilliant enough to become a
potential competitive threat.[5] Obviously, problems of cadre power
absorb most of the Politburo members' time so that they hardly ever
get down to a serious analysis of political questions, economic
problems, and proposals for change. When they do, the results are
more often than not partial solutions while general social problems
on a nationwide level escape their attention.[6] All the working papers,
reports, and proposals that are submitted during the sessions of the
Politburo are mostly prepared by the central party secretariat.
Considering the concept of the party's leadership, the volume of the
reading material is so overwhelming that the Politburo members are
seldom able to carefully study in advance all the prepared papers,
not to mention to analyze, discuss, and prepare alternatives. Most
Politburo members have their own apparatus prepare in advance the
statements and additions that they are planning to present at the
sessions. Thus, after mostly formal discussions, this important
organism takes politically highly relevant decisions that in fact have
been made by an irresponsible and bureaucratic apparatus.[7]

Since the political "representatives" understand very little about
the increasingly complicated economical and political situation and
since they are not able to cope with the flood of information, there is
very little they can do to avoid making erroneous decisions on the
basis of drafts submitted by the anonymous bureaucratic apparatus.
This implies that they have to concentrate all the more on consolidating their position of power, which may suffer from the inevitable
accumulation of mistakes and shortcomings. The conditions of

becoming a successful politician or cadre are not so much professional qualifications and the ability to solve and explain problems or
popularity with the people, but certain questionable political characteristics. Only a person capable of conforming for many years to the
most powerful men while efficiently dealing with current and potential adversaries (mostly by playing on the "class position") and
capable of deceiving the people and willing to make sacrifices for the
benefit of his political ambitions can be sure of succeeding in a
political career and of getting a promotion to one of the highest
leadership positions. These very qualifications and characteristics
are valued as proof of a determined and dedicated stand for socialism, whereas any demonstration of strong emotions is rejected as
petty-bourgeois sentimentality.

The ability of exploiting people for one's own benefit can take
various disguises. One way is to get into, or to keep in, leading and
attractive positions people who have never fulfilled the necessary
professional requirements, or whose qualifications are not good
enough for these positions. This means that these people will be all
the more dependent on the person who is responsible for their
promotion or who maintains them in their positions. More often than
not they become willing puppets. To ensure absolute obedience, it is
sometimes sufficient to remove someone who has dared to express an
opinion differing from the one presented by the secretary or another
powerful functionary. Another possibility to promote personal
power is to exploit personal differences between certain functionaries. Many of the innumerable reorganizations within the administrative apparatus (mergers or divisions of ministries, and so forth)
have been used to fill certain positions or to get rid of certain people.
These tactics usually generate an atmosphere of constant anxiety
and uneasiness among the bureaucrats and help motivate their ever
ready eagerness to conform and obey.

A system of selection for leading functionaries from the top all
the way down to the base in the enterprises and villages using the
exclusive criteria of power, obedience, conformism, and deference
necessarily results in a low achievement level and average, as well
as below-average, leadership. Opportunistic adaptation and lack of
principles become integral characteristics of individual behavior.
Careerism takes a specific form: not people with initiative and an
innovative mind advance in their career but those who are careful
always to say "yes," execute orders, believe in authority, and do their
jobs without asking questions. The skill of reporting to one's superiors exactly what they want to hear and to avoid mentioning anything
they do not want to admit gradually leads to such bias in the

information system that the leadership is far removed from the real situation, from the actual mood and opinion of the people, and consequently feels confirmed in its own subjective concepts and illusions.

Similar to what happens within the party, the manipulation of cadres elsewhere is covered up by "democratic" elections. For all village, district, county, and central "elections," candidates are selected by the party secretariats and entered on the list of candidates by the responsible institutions. In countries where other political parties formally exist as, for example, the National Front, the Communist Party apparatus nominates *reliable* and *conformist* representatives of these parties—and sometimes even "nonparty" candidates—who are then entered in the list by way of "agreements" with these parties. The entire political activity of these "parties" is controlled by the National Front's secretariats, whose members are bureaucrats reporting de facto to the Communist Party apparatus. Any attempts by these parties to formulate their own politics or to act as an opposition party would immediately be repressed as proof of anticommunist activity.

In solemnly and propagandistically well-staged "elections," the population then has the possibility of accepting the listed candidates. There is no option among several lists of candidates as they would be prepared by various independent organizations. The formal rejection of certain candidates by entering other names cannot qualify as a real election process since the voters have no opportunity of consulting with each other beforehand, and of organizing the nomination of countercandidates. It does not even serve any purpose just to reject a suggested candidate because only the responsible and carefully chosen bureaucrat has the means of controlling the actual election results. Also, the entire election procedure is so closely watched over by spies that the voters do not even make use of the theoretical possibility of rejecting a candidate, knowing that the election results are determined in advance. The voters cast their ballots just the way they are. In this way it is made sure that "free" elections always result in 99 percent of the votes cast for the suggested candidates—the expression of the people's "moral-political unity."

Once elected to the Soviets, the deputies will be able to implement only the program that has been set up by the party and that provides the deputies with concrete guidelines for passing the necessary laws. All legislative activity is dedicated to formalizing party decisions and party directives that no deputy and no commission of the Soviets can afford to bypass. Meetings of the deputies with their voters are primarily of an agitational nature destined to mobilize the participants for the fulfillment of plans and the increase in production. The deputies are fully aware of the fact that they cannot bring about essential changes in the lives of their constituents, or in the system and its shortcomings. The voters are equally aware of this situation.

If on the occasion of such meetings the voters take enough courage to file a complaint concerning delivery shortages, poor quality of consumer products, housing, and so forth, the deputy may at best refer this criticism to the responsible enterprise or any other institution. Although he may be successful in obtaining certain improvements, he will not be able to remove the causes for the repeated shortcomings.

N. W. Podgorny came very close to demagogism when in an election speech he talked about the "extension of democracy" as demonstrated by the fact that the "voters delegate orders to their future deputies," and that "of the 1,700,000 projects accepted by the Soviets in the course of the past four years, nearly one and a half million had been executed."[8] However, Podgorny did not say in which way these orders and projects had been carried out and what had been done to avoid repeated criticism about poor quality, shortages, bureaucratic delays and red tape, missing spare parts and repair facilities for agricultural machinery, and so forth.[9]

Democracy is a formality at best as long as a deputy is just considered a "collector of complaints" and "mailman" who does not ask basic political questions, does not inquire into the causes of repeated shortcomings, and abstains from criticizing the political leadership. A special section within the party apparatus that is responsible for the election of deputies makes sure that none of these deputies even so much as reflect on such issues, in other words, that every one of them remains just an obedient "mailman." As with all official positions, that of deputy in the Soviets (Supreme Soviet as well as district soviets) is reserved for those activists or conformists who fully endorse the "leading role of the party" and are willing to faithfully follow its lead.

Obviously, this kind of cadre politics is designed to ensure that the Communist Party bureaucracy places its followers and abiding activists in all the key positions in order to be in total control of the entire population. Why don't the people rebel against such manipulation and tutelage by eliminating the communist bureaucracy from power? A partial answer to this question can be given when examining the other instrument used by the communist power establishment.

REPRESSION AND CORRUPTION

Repression no longer refers to the members of the former "class of exploiters" which for all practical purposes no longer exist in the Soviet Union, and in the other Eastern European countries has been reduced to a small number of old and resigned people who wield neither power nor influence. Repression today is a fact to be reckoned with by all those who are not willing to be completely subdued by the system, who insist on expressing their opposition, criticism, or indignation regarding the party bureaucracy's concepts and interests, and who may even resort to active or passive resistance. Obviously, the people most suffering from repression are members of the working class whose "liberation from any exploitation and repression" the "proletarian" state was supposed to achieve. The fact that the dictatorship of the proletariat has resulted in the liquidation of mainly working class people seems like a bad historical joke.[10] Marx's prophecy has long since lost any validity: that the state will be eliminated after the liquidation of the last class of exploiters to be replaced by a common administration of societal interests. On the contrary, the bureaucratic apparatus increases with each year at the same rate as the entire range of repressive instruments, such as police, courts, prisons, concentration camps, and so forth.

Among all the repressive systems that have existed in the course of history, the communist system is one of the best organized and most efficient. When compared to other totalitarian repressive systems, it appears that its strength resides in the complexity of repressive methods interacting with the precision of clockwork. A complete range of administrative means of repression is available for silencing, in one way or the other, anyone who attempts to express dissatisfaction or differing political opinions: ordinary police methods including questioning and threats, trials for antigovernment activities, long prison terms, staged-show trials including torture and death sentences as a warning to the masses, psychological destruction of personalities who cannot be put to trial because of their popularity and who are instead declared mentally ill and locked away in psychiatric institutions, quiet deportation of millions of people "under cover of darkness,"[11] organized assassinations of popular figures that are then blamed on class enemies, a charge that is exploited as an excuse for starting mass terror and purges. There are educational institutions and special military service for the sons of state enemies, labor and concentration camps where the inmates are gradually eliminated through the combined effects of hard labor, hunger, illness, and punitive actions. Even though the successors of Stalin and other communist leaders can no longer afford to indulge to the same degree in mass terror and mass liquidation as Stalin himself, the repressive methods described above have been, and still are, applied though in more subtle and less sensational ways. They are designed not only to silence a few political opponents but primarily to discourage the great number of those who could be tempted to engage in oppositional activities.

Although Stalin's repressive methods were criticized by Khrushchev at the Twentieth Party Congress of the Communist Party of the Soviet Union, and although efforts are still being made today to pretend that these methods have been eliminated at the same time as the Stalin cult, administrative repression continues to exist under the cover of legality. But the fact has to be considered that although "antigovernment activity" is a charge defined by very specific laws, these laws allow for an extremely wide range of interpretation. Also, in all political trials whose presiding judges are party members, charges and sentences are discussed and decided in advance in the party secretariats, and foreign journalists are practically never admitted to these trials. Therefore, even today any legal procedure is as efficient a repressive instrument as it was during Stalin's reign.[12]

In all the Eastern European countries the first to be silenced and liquidated were the devoted members of the noncommunist political parties and all oppositional groups that tried to fight off the ascent of a communist dictatorship. The noncommunist public, obviously the overwhelming majority of the people, was excluded from any kind of political activity to such a degree that one could justifiably speak of political emasculation. To give just one example, in Czechoslovakia, which had the relatively largest Communist Party, party membership in 1968, the year of the highest enrollment, was only about ten percent of the population. Only a very limited number of nonparty members devoted to the communist cause were manipulated by the Communist Party into various official positions for the purpose of giving the appearance that the noncommunist segment of the population was in fact represented. In purely quantitative terms this, of course, was a joke.

Under these circumstances, the noncommunist opposition obviously was in no position to be politically active in a legal way. The slightest attempts at any illegal political activity, even in the form of distributing oppositional information material, have been, and are, severely punished with stiff prison sentences. This naturally results in a situation where occasional opposition movements can develop only within the Communist Party. These movements became more or less representative of those noncommunist segments of the population that did not agree with the Communist Party bureaucracy's political line. For some time, such opposition groups existing within the party were able to cover up their activities relatively easily and to operate in favor of various reforms or liberalization measures. For the most part, however, they were, and are, destroyed like any noncommunist opposition the very moment their demands contradict and therefore threaten the basic interests of the party bureaucracy.

In order to discourage other party members from engaging in such "dangerous" oppositional activities within the party, the members of these movements were each time "unmasked as the worst enemy" and severely punished. And still there have always been opposition and reform movements within the Communist Parties of the Eastern European countries that in full knowledge of the risks involved have tried in various ways to promote liberalization and democratization. These groups were formed by ordinary party members but very often also included members of various elected party organs or institutions. They mostly belonged to the party intelligentsia, which honestly believed in the officially proclaimed ideology of an overall liberation of the working class and which had not lost touch with the population. When these communists begin to realize the total contradiction between the words and the actions of the leading communist bureaucrats as well as the system's negative consequences for the population, when they—often in shock—find themselves free of their former illusions, they engage in a desperate fight for basic changes in the system. Time and again, in all Eastern European countries, hundreds and thousands of communists have tried to fight the party's power apparatus and its bureaucratic leaders. They have tried to achieve their goal with open criticism, by organizing factions and illegal associations, with desperate revolts, or through long and patient efforts to achieve certain reforms. And time and again, they have been brutally suppressed by their own party's bureaucracy, or by the military forces of their "socialist" neighbors' united party bureaucracies.

For the most part, the victims of repression were communists who during the years of capitalism or during the years of the Communist Party's struggle for power had joined the party and later were liquidated by the corrupted party bureaucracy.[13]

But all these revolts, within as well as outside the party, are not repressed only with the help of administrative methods. There are other means, such as public defamation, libel, scandals, name calling, and accusations, not to mention the widely used method of economic repression, a communist speciality never quite matched by any other repressive system.

The act of publicly designating an enemy is a tool of repression that ever since Stalin has been expertly handled by all communist dictators. A very effective means of intimidation is the labeling of a person in a party speech, in a party newspaper article, on radio or television by referring to this person with names such as "enemy of the people," "deviationist," "cosmopolitan," "opportunist," "revisionist," "agent of imperialism," and so forth. People know that there is no defense against such defamation. While the powerful party official is not required to substantiate his accusation, the accused has no possibility of publishing any proof to the contrary, not to mention of filing a charge against the libelist. But he can be certain that the allegation alone will bring him harrassment and inconvenience in regard to his social and economic position, that he will be suspected and watched by all the functionaries and bureaucrats and especially by the state police. The act of name calling can mean the first of a series of administrative measures: as far as the bureaucratic apparatus is concerned, the accused becomes an outcast whose social "death" may have begun.[14]

Economic repression ranges from subtle harassment at the place of work, transfer to inferior jobs, and nonpromotions to terminations, for which there is no appeal on the ground of loss of political trustworthiness. In a society where all enterprises and institutions are state-owned and companies hire new employees only on the basis of cadre information regarding the candidate's previous employment record, the loss of a job for political reasons can mean lifelong persecution. Whatever his qualifications, this person will only be able to find lesser paid and little respected jobs, he will be fired again and again and probably go unemployed for months at a time. This puts him in a situation where he constantly risks being arrested for vagrancy and ending up in a labor camp. The children of persons who have lost their political "trustworthiness," who have been expelled from the party, or who have been tried for political crimes do not qualify for college level education.[15] Thus, blood feud becomes part of a system that its representatives advocate as being a "scientifically based and progressive system." In reality, however, threatening the children's future represents a means of pressure that has more leverage on many people than physical repression against their own person.

It goes without saying that such an extended and well-organized system of repression is provided with a unique spy network. All party members are committed to report to the party organs "hostile" statements made by coworkers, neighbors, and friends. Even though only a limited percentage of party members actually engages in spying, the number of informants is still high enough. In addition to these voluntary "ideological" informants, there is an unusually large staff of informants operating within each enterprise and institution, unknown to their coworkers and paid by the state police. Also, in Eastern European countries the janitors of apartment buildings are almost invariably police informants who are required to regularly report on tenants' behavior, opinions, visitors, and so forth. Not to put out the flag on time on official holidays may be enough reason for the janitor to denounce a tenant with whom he is not very good friends.

Thus, the state police has become the most important center of administrative repression, having at its disposition an extensive information network including the most modern bugging and spying devices, using the cadre files covering even the slightest suspect, practicing sophisticated interrogation methods and physical as well as psychological means of repression. Police power increases with its methods and information, and with the persecution of persons of differing opinions this power exceeds the limits of a mere instrument of the party bureaucracy. Very often the police apparatus itself initiates allegations, arrests and accusations that may even be directed at powerful members of the party apparatus and lead to their downfall and elimination. There are bureaucrats who thrive on people's fears, who purposely trigger anxieties in order to consolidate their own powerful positions until they extend beyond any control. These people even manipulate courts and prosecutors into a state of dependency [16] and use compromising material to put political pressure on even the highest party functionary. The existence of this kind of repression and spying system generates a constant feeling of "insecurity and anxiety"[17] in the populations of all East European countries. This, in turn, leads to a fear of expressing one's opinion, to self-censoring, pretending, and lying. Many people have learned to lead a double life: as an officially happy, well-conformed, and apolitical person on the outside, and a privately frustrated, angry, and even hateful individual on the inside who hides his true personality from his closest relatives, including even a spouse, and from his children, who could be tempted to talk in school.[18]

In the same way as in the fascist countries which the communists like to criticize, the great majority of the Eastern Europeans are leading a double life. In these countries, too, the necessity to hide one's true nature, opinions, and values is leading to increasing frustration, alienation, schizophrenia, and suicidal tendencies. Obviously, it is the intellectuals who suffer most from this situation, whereas the majority of the working-class people turn into politically indifferent citizens who live for their private concerns and interests such as weekend homes, gardening, sports events, and so forth.

The regime does not mind this kind of individualization as long as the workers meet their job requirements as planned and controlled by the enterprise, and as long as they participate in the various public events, such as May Day parades, enterprise assemblies, and so forth. All the regime wants are obedient robots. Only very occasionally do the political bureaucrats expect a public demonstration of "mass enthusiasm" for the benefit of foreign observers. Since the workers want to be left alone, they quickly learn to perform this kind of traditional duty. They know exactly what is going on; they know how the plans are fulfilled, which are the personal politics of the different functionaries. They know who watches, spies, and informs, who during the May Day parades registers the presence and "enthusiasm" or, in the assemblies, the attitudes and votes. They are prepared to go along formally in order to be able to have a certain privacy that is worth living for. Thus, the "socialist" liberation has created a sense of alienation to a degree that the capitalist system of exploitation has not been able to match. However, if a system is to be maintained without the support of a majority of the population, or even at the cost of suppressing large segments of the population, there have to be definite advantages for the suppressors and especially for the leading bureaucrats to be willing to exercise this kind of activity and thus commit themselves to the system. Therefore, corruption is always the other side of the coin in any repressive system. For the greater the shortcomings, the lacking consumer products, and the unsatisfied needs of the population, the easier it is to corrupt the leading officials.

In the Stalinist system, the party apparatus as well as the most important ministries (defense, state police, and so forth) had, and still have, their own shops, mostly in the same buildings for security's sake, where the bureaucrats could buy everything that was not or rarely available in the ordinary stores. After World War II, this arrangement was adopted by the other "socialist" countries. The preferential allocation of apartments—which still are in short supply—and later of automobiles to all top level functionaries is being practiced to this very day.

For members of the party bureaucracy there are special weekend and vacation homes or even entire areas offering the best in supplies and services and other amenities. The systematic categorizing of such recreation facilities for different levels of functionaries[19] is designed to create strong career incentives. In addition, higher party officials have access to recreation facilities outside their own countries that offer all kinds of luxuries in choice surroundings.

Stalin had introduced a system of special rewards for members of the Politburo. He personally distributed substantial amounts of money in envelopes—and therefore called "couverts"—according to the "behavior" of the "rewarded" person. These rewards were a particularly efficient means of corruption since they were granted in addition to the normally high salaries, were given secretly, and were nontaxable. And they were handed over by Stalin himself. Novotny among other communist leaders adopted this custom for his party.[20]

The most common and probably most effective means of corruption is the systematic transformation from ordinary worker to bureaucrat. A person without any formal education who has been able to escape the exhausting life of a factory worker only by getting some party schooling or enrolling in special college courses for workers will do anything to keep his position as an influential bureaucrat for the rest of his life.[21] Considering how attractive the "white collar" is in societies where the bureaucracy serves the rich bourgeoisie or aristocracy, how much more desirable will be the position of a ruling party bureaucrat in a communist country. The "chosen" inevitably become the most loyal supporters of the system that offers them such unique opportunities.

This kind of direct corruption of high-level and influential functionaries by means of generous remunerations, fringe benefits, and prospects for even greater advantages, and, last but not least, the prestige of holding a bureaucratic position within the party apparatus ensures the communist system a ruling class of great reliability. Supported by this kind of bureaucratic class, such a system can be maintained over decades while suppressing any opposition, reform movement, or revolt. The only important factor is that the party bureaucracy is able to draw on a secure reserve for recruiting and for carrying out specific tasks. The reserve, in this case, in the Communist Party itself.

The problem, however, lies with the ordinary party member, and in none of the East European countries can the entire Communist Party be considered a reliable pillar of the regime. The majority of the ordinary party members, particularly those who joined the party for ethical-idealistic considerations and out of a genuine belief in socialism, gradually become strongly disillusioned. As soon as these people are aware of the total contradiction of ideological propaganda and actual reality, they retreat into political passivity and emotional adversity to the bureaucracy, resulting especially in the case of workers leaving the party. Or these people commit themselves to some underground opposition movement that obviously is consequential only in the case of intellectual party members holding an important position within the existing power system.[22] However, there is a sufficiently large number of party members, especially in the USSR, who have not yet discovered the truth behind the illusion and who are still being taken in by official information and propaganda. Although many of these communists, if they are honest with themselves, are quite aware of the system's shortcomings and of their coworkers' dissatisfaction, they are not capable of recognizing the essential causes as originating in the system itself. The great majority of these people believe in Marx's and Lenin's great thoughts and ideals and are more or less convinced that the party leadership is concerned with the people's well-being. Shortcomings are explained by bad planning and control at the ministerial level and those "lazying" bureaucrats. This kind of communist still attempts to address criticism to the state apparatus by writing letters to the party leadership—which the party bureaucracy not only could not care less about but often actually welcome. Or these communists are convinced that the cause of all the existing difficulties lies with the "imperialists who are threatening the Soviet Union, thus forcing her to invest so heavily in armaments." Such reasoning is very widespread in party members in the USSR but less typical of the other Eastern European countries.

Obviously, a great many ordinary party members joined the party merely to make a career as a functionary without any ideological motivations at all. From their ranks the party recruits the majority of its activists, informants, and police spies, as well as its candidates for promotion. However, although these "future bureaucrats" are important to the bureaucratic establishment, they cannot replace those communists who have not yet abused their coworkers, cotenants, and so forth. The informants and "zealots" normally have no political influence with their coworkers; they are too well known for what they are and therefore carefully avoided. This leaves only those communists who are not yet discredited in this regard to act as liaison between the party apparatus and the population. And since the apparatus is interested in winning over the population for various socially required activities not only under pressure and fear but by voluntary decision, it will always try and keep a certain number of communists "by conviction" and particularly ordinary workers within the party membership. This becomes increasingly difficult to achieve as fewer and fewer ordinary workers who have nothing to lose and are not as hard pressured as intellectuals avoid joining the party.[23] This trend demonstrates very clearly what the worker thinks of the party and of the entire system.

However, the apparatus cannot afford to stop exerting ideological influence on party members and on at least a certain percentage of the population.[24] First, it is essential to provide the party bureaucracy with ideological justification and moral excuses for their activities, including their acts of repression. Second, a certain percentage of ordinary party members and of the noncommunist population is likely to be irritated or neutralized by ideological influence. This situation explains the importance of the third element in the mechanism of power: the ideological monopoly.

IDEOLOGICAL MONOPOLY

In a system where press, radio, television, publishing, and so forth are state-owned and centrally controlled and manipulated, the mass media are obviously at the service of the power bureaucracy, its goals, and interests. The population, after years of negative experience, has learned to be wary when reading the newspaper. But under the impact of specific and recurring information and permanent one-sided propaganda, the public is no longer able to assess the real state of its societal makeup and the extent of certain shortcomings. The people no longer have any means of balancing the system's advantages against its disadvantages, since there are no possibilities of comparing their own with other societies. In short, the population is at the total mercy of the power mechanism that controls the mass media.

The power elite of bureaucratic communism has learned to use the instruments of public ideological influence to such perfection that it exceeds all previous totalitarian systems. By staffing mass media and public opinion-forming organs with high-level and reliable cadres who are loyal to the regime, the information system has been completely subordinated and deformed. The ideological cadres are in constant contact with the party secretariats, which periodically as well as for certain special events provide guidelines and concrete directives in view of the attitude to take toward specific issues. In addition, the directors and editors-in-chief have full responsibility for all publications and programs issued by their departments, which are closely controlled by the responsible section of the party secretariat. A cadre's slightest deviation from the party line attracts immediate criticism, and repeated criticism leads to the loss of his job.

Particularly after the experience with the Czechoslovakian reform movement, the system of ideological leadership and control of all cadres has been reorganized and perfected in most Eastern European countries and especially in the USSR. After almost ten years of patient and systematic information activity in the ideological sphere, as well as the careful introduction of progressive reformers into some editorial staffs, the Czechoslovakian reformers had succeeded in gaining increasing support for their movement of reform and opposition to the Novotny regime. The Stalinist party bureaucracy has drawn its conclusion from this experience: in addition to an overall mass purge, all newly recruited cadres have to meet extensive requirements. Preference is now given to those cadres who may lack certain special knowledge or skills but are politically reliable. Very often these people have been committed to the party's services because of various discrediting material that would otherwise be used against them.[25]

It is not the task of the mass media to provide the consumer with authentic information from the source of events but to select and present available information with the purpose of conditioning people's attitude toward specific political goals and thus securing maximum support for the political leadership. This means that information has to be suppressed, especially when it relates to failures and shortcomings of the socialist system, to critical and nonconformist opinions, to foreign events that threaten to play down domestic achievements, to contradictions occurring within the party, to expressions of dissatisfaction among the people, and so forth. On the other hand, any information has to be played up that mentions special achievements, spontaneous demonstrations of popular approval, and support of party politics, that points to the growth and strength of socialist production, or to any proof of international support in favor of the socialist system, the advantages and superior features of this system as compared with capitalism, and so forth.

In order to avoid that domestic information activity is discredited by facts from abroad, it is necessary to block the inflow of foreign news by prohibiting or limiting the import and free sale of foreign newspapers, by severely censuring the use and distribution of news, articles, and books coming from abroad, by jamming foreign radio programs, and so forth. Strict limitation on foreign travel serves the same purpose.

Obviously, it does not imply that the regime never admits to any mistakes and shortcomings, for such a policy would make for ineffective information and propaganda. On the contrary, an apparent objectivity is created by occasional criticism and complaints expressed by either the political leadership itself or by members of the working class as published in letters to the editor. However, the dosage of this aspect of publishing has to be carefully administered to ensure that shortcomings appear relatively negligible and temporary in the context of the overall impressive achievement. Also, the integral characteristics of the system must not be questioned and the causes of repeated failures must not be uncovered. In short, information has to reinforce the system and must not create any doubt of its "superiority" over all other systems.

The same reasoning results in a kind of propaganda that is not much more than a stereotyped enumeration of achievements supported by simplified facts, such as data on overall production growth or preferential lines of products, compared to prerevolutionary years, while carefully avoiding any data or comparison that could minimize certain "achievements." Thus, there simply are no comparative data on consumption patterns in Western countries, on per capita income, on average working hours that a worker has to put in for the purchase of certain consumer goods, on return on capital, and so forth. Propaganda material has to demonstrate the socialist system's superiority over capitalism and to praise its unique progressiveness in problem solving. The way this kind of informative material negates the existence of any problems at all seems downright ridiculous. The "tasks of socialist construction" are achieved with such ease, and difficulties are admitted as exceptions, as initial "childhood diseases" that the workers are learning to cope with." Developments such as price increases that are typical of both systems are termed "integral negative results of capitalism" on the one hand, and "a necessary step taken by the state to even out partial disproportions due to nonfulfillment of plans by a few enterprises" on the other hand. The policy of fighting shortcomings by educating the workers with the help of positive examples and not by public criticism leads to a compulsive search for "good examples," to the primitive selection and idealizing of workers' heroes, and praising of "work records."

Similar propagandistic excesses are expected from the "social sciences." This discipline is not required to point out actual existing contradictions and problems within the society or to suggest solutions since this kind of scientific research would necessarily result in criticism of many decisions taken by the leading political organs. Although scientifically well-founded suggestions for improvement could be beneficial to society, the danger would exist that in view of the power struggle at the top these proposals are used by one functionary against another. Therefore, all scientific knowledge is suppressed in an effort to avoid revealing the system's basic and general shortcomings that would jeopardize the power of the entire ruling class. Reform proposals will always be "antisocialist and hostile" since anything that undermines the ruling elite's powerful position is by definition antisocialist and antistate. Consequently, the social sciences have degenerated into delivering apologetics of bureaucratic socialism as the one and only "socialism."

The formulation of economic reform theories in the CSSR under the Novotny regime had only been possible on the basis of many years of courageous and exhausting preparatory work by economists, statisticians, and business administrators who gradually achieved a systematic broadening of objective economic information and statistical data. How much effort had gone into just eliminating the secret classification of data on the gross national product. How much energy had to be put into obtaining the statistical compilation of data relating to the development of prices, real income, and so forth and how much courage and integrity on the part of scientists was needed to prepare comparative studies uncovering—against the wish of the party apparatus—the fact that the Czechoslovakian people's standard of living was far behind that of the Western industrial countries. Obviously, these studies had not been published before the "Prague Spring" but their existence alone and the internal distribution of all analyses and comparative data helped accelerate the evolution of new theories and essential reform proposals.

However, this was an extraordinary period. Due to rapidly deteriorating economic conditions in the early 1960s and the resulting dissatisfaction of the Czech workers on the one hand, and the long and patient effort of honest and progressive people on the other hand, the incapable and politically discredited Novotny regime was forced to make certain concessions in view of a more liberal and objective approach by its sociologists. Truthful revelations in one sector paved the way for scientific honesty in others. Scientists, artists, and publicists slowly succeeded in paralyzing a dull and apologetic party propaganda machine, although investigations, punishment, and persecution did not let up and the party bureaucracy attempted to increase its police power.

Such extraordinary times and such an ideological breakthrough are not characteristic of the general state of the social sciences in the countries of bureaucratic socialism. On the contrary, the typical situation is the strict control of all scientific institutions by the party apparatus and the direct evaluation of their activities and achievements according to the apparatus' standards of political "purity." In the CSSR, too, the suppression of the reform movement resulted in the most severe measures applied in research institutes, colleges, editorial staffs, publishing houses, and so forth. The directors and leading personnel of these institutions were replaced, some institutes were simply closed, others lost the majority of their staff. Humiliating public autocriticism and declarations of conformism were forced on many people and all the involved reformers were detached to do "ordinary physical work." Today, only "scientific" work that conforms to the political needs of the bureaucrats has any chance of being published.

In the educational field, from elementary school through college and vocational training institutes, surveillance and control by the party apparatus are particularly tight. Education in the spirit of Marxist-Lenist ideology does not imply helping a child grow up to become an independent, critically and creatively thinking individual but teaches parrotlike repeating and memorizing of dogmatic beliefs. To doubt the veracity of these doctrines is equivalent to antisocialist heresy. In total contradiction to Marx's demand for continuous skepticism regarding any theories, for permanent confrontation with reality, and for revision of outdated or unrealistic theorems, the young generation in the "socialist" countries is being brainwashed into believing that any examination of the Marxist-Leninist theory is equivalent to a betrayal of socialism. The most recent recognized revisions of Marxism were those made by Lenin;[26] however, they are not presented expressly as revisions but as the logical Leninist continuation of Marxism. Today, any deviation from these accepted and eternally valid theories is prohibited and subject to inquisitorial prosecution.

The terms "socialism" and "capitalism" are elevated to dogmas aiming at creating an effect similar to the religious concepts of "God" and "devil." Although the meaning of the term "socialism" raises the most essential questions any person striving for knowledge could ask, and although it requires a continuous analysis of the system's actual development, of its objectively inherent contexts, its contradictions, and achievements, the young generation is not allowed to give any independent thought to the meaning of socialism. The interpretation of key sociological terms is the exclusive reserve of the official party ideologists. They will always limit themselves to enumerating the most abstract characteristics. Their actual realities, contradictions, advantages, and shortcomings are, again, not open to examination. "Socialism is a system which has eliminated any exploitation and suppression of the workers"; "socialism is a system which is based on social ownership of all means of production and a planned, proportional development of production"; "socialism guarantees the fastest development of productive forces and the improvement of the population's material and cultural standard of living"; "socialism by means of the dictatorship of the prolerariat guarantees the most extensive democratic system for the working individual." Anybody who wants to learn about the meaning of "socialism" has to be satisfied with these and similar dogmas, and it is by means of these platitudes that the teachers in the socialist schools have to educate their students in the spirit of Marxism-Leninism.

If a scientist or college professor who is a party member discovers contradictions between the officially presented theory and practical reality, he is well advised to keep this knowledge to himself unless he wants to risk being discredited as a revisionist. Likewise, an economist who knows that central planning is not the right approach to ensuring sufficient production development but on the contrary results in anarchy and losses, and who would therefore be tempted to stress the necessity of replacing central planning by other planning mechanisms more likely to secure the socially required production proportions would, by speaking out, threaten not only the dogma of "socialist planning regularity." Above all, he would represent a real danger to the planning system, which is the basis of the party apparatus' overwhelming economic power. For this very reason, a socialist economist who expresses doubts has to be persecuted more severely than a bourgeois economist who rejects socialism as such and praises the advantages of capitalism. The critical and innovative socialist economist becomes a dangerous heretic who has "signed a pact with capitalism" and who therefore must be prevented from exercising any ideological and political influence on practical "socialism,"

The accusation against the "revisionist" theoreticians is not based on realistic arguments, and the arguments used by theoreticians termed "revisionists" are simply ignored by the dogmatic party ideologists. If, for example, a socialist economist, by analyzing the system of state ownership in Eastern European countries, disclosed the basic shortcomings of this form of ownership (bureaucratization, alienation of the workers, inefficiency, and so forth) and therefore suggested another form of collective ownership, he would be regarded as a so-called "enemy of collective ownership" and branded as anti-socialist. His arguments and data used to prove the fact that in reality state ownership is not people's ownership are ignored and meet with the laconic assertion that the search for differing forms of collective ownership does not conform to Marxism-Leninism. The way in which all new theoretical discoveries are refuted on the basis of the established Marxist-Leninist criterion demonstrates the absolutely dogmatic acceptance of this theory and the political resistance to any theoretical development. There is absolutely no ability and no will to accept criticism if it collides with bureaucratic power interests, no matter how well founded it is by irrefutable facts.

When an independent opinion is voiced at a college or at a research institute, or when certain ideas from abroad that the party apparatus deems to be politically dangerous to the system begin to infiltrate an Eastern European country, party ideologists are invariably made to write a so-called "polemic" in the form of an ideological dissertation or a book review. The political purpose of such a "polemic" is self-evident. There is no intention of examining whether or not a certain new opinion is right, if one of its elements may be acceptable, and which data might be simplified or wrong. The aim is to demonstrate that this particular opinion does not correspond to the established political line and therefore has to be rejected—which immediately eliminates the Marxist criterion of truth. As soon as somebody expresses opinions which, according to bureaucratic evaluation, do not conform with those of the political leadership but are critical of this leadership or even point to basic failures of the system, these opinions have to be condemned. The way in which this is done depends on the desired effect but the demagogic procedure is well-known. The rejected opinion is distorted, essential arguments that cannot be proven wrong are deleted, sentences are quoted out of context, the author is probably said to have expressed completely different opinions than what he really said, and so forth. All these maneuvers are aimed at unmasking the author as an "enemy," "anti-Marxist," and "revisionist," therefore, it would only be dangerous to correctly repeat his opinions in a factual discussion. Communist ideologists have a deep-rooted fear that certain practical or theoretical contradictions in "socialism" discovered by some theoretician may be spread by public discussion. So they try to warn the people not to even read the criticized works and not to listen to any rejected opinions.

The entire campaign conducted against the revisionists in the CSSR is based solely on the accusation that these people wanted to eliminate socialism and reintroduce capitalism. All articles, books, and reports written after the military intervention of 1968 against the revisionists were naturally based on the assumption that "socialism" could not possibly have any other meaning than what the party bureaucracy ascribed to it. Therefore, any attempt at changing bureaucratic state ownership or central planning would be equivalent to starting an "antisocialist counterrevolution." As for the reform proposals themselves, their justification or nonjustification could no longer be discussed in either speeches or in writing. The only element common to all accusations was a description of the "counterrevolutionary conspiracy," a list of all "antisocialist" articles, declarations, and books published by the revisionists, but not one word about their actual proposals, arguments, and goals.

The complete misinterpretation of current Czechoslovakian viewpoints by party ideologists aiming at discrediting the reformers as antisocialist and anti-working class traitors is enough proof of the still existing Stalinist propaganda.[27] Instead of refuting these realistic analyses, arguments, and proposals and thereby confirming the validity of the official concept of socialism, the party attributes to these reformers certain intentions that they never advocated or expressed. Everything goes in such a campaign: the most infamous lies as to these people's opinions; personal scandalizations involving alleged ties to "West German revanchists," to "Zionist conspirators," and so forth. This kind of propaganda whose authors cannot be held responsible for their allegations is proof enough that nothing has changed over the years. In the same way that Stalinist propaganda for decades has slandered in the most infamous manner the Trotsky-ites, Bukharites, and others in order to discredit them in the eyes of several generations as the "most dangerous conspirators and coun-terrevolutionaries" whose real opinions and activities were best forgotten and whose names were better not mentioned, the Czech reformers are vilified today in their country. How is this propaganda different from the Stalinist one that had been rejected with just as much propaganda not so long ago? Traitors have to be created and their concepts of "socialism" have to be eradicated from the minds of the people. "For or against socialism" therefore is made to mean the same as being "for or against the interpretation of socialism by the party apparatus," resulting in the systematic crippling of indepen-dent and critical thinking. What happens is the total perversion of the "scientific truthfulness" of Marxist theory into an unrealistic religion: its content represents the "absolute truth" which, with all administrative means available, has to be forced on the people for their own good.[28]

A great number of teachers are fully aware of the unreality transmitted by the officially prescribed teaching material. They know very well the conflict that this situation creates in the con-science of the young generation which they have to educate. How-ever, the permanent supervision in all the schools not only in the form of outside inspection but above all by means of spying and reporting from eager activists, student functionaries of the commu-nist youth organizations, and so forth forces almost all teachers and professors to become hypocrites and to adapt their teaching to the system's requirements. For, a teacher who looks suspicious to the educational division of the party bureaucracy will sooner or later be dispensed from teaching.[29] This, of course, results in being excluded for life from exercising one's profession, and therefore most teachers try to conform and teach the required subjects as formally and detached as possible.

In the area of education, too, we find the typical bureaucratic setup involving all kinds of administrative formalities. The most important requirement is to deliver proof of one's "loyalty" to superiors and of one's commitment to an education in the "spirit of Marxism." The central bureaucracy could not and does not intend to investigate the actual change in conscience of the "educated"; what counts is the quantity of educational actions. Whether elementary school, college, or party school, the responsible bureaucrat is only interested in the annual statistics showing the number of "Marxist-Leninist" conferences, courses, seminars, and lectures delivered, and the number of students attending, as evidence of the desired and prescribed activity. What really happens in the minds of the people does not interest the bureaucrat for he is only responsible for the "activity." Teachers have to bring proof of their "activities," students of their participation. As for the exams, the only requirements are memorized cliches bearing no relation to reality.

The long list of prohibited books and authors that has at all times been part of the communist system and is mandatory for scientific institutions and others can only be compared to the book bans of fascist regimes or with medieval inquisition practices. Banned books are quietly removed from the libraries and destroyed. Many books that had been written and published during the Novotny years are today prohibited and have been removed from all libraries and institutions. Typically, for the bureaucracy it is the destruction of the books that counts, because the reflection of truth is more dangerous than the actual reality.

As for artistic activities, they are only legitimate if they serve the immediate political goals and interests of socialism. The arts should be committed to winning the workers for the fulfillment of socialist ideals. They are also expected to contribute to an education in the spirit of socialist moral principles and to the fight against the enemies of socialism and all those forces that undermine the people's unity. According to their "political vocation," the arts not only have to be constantly educational but are expected to agitate the masses by use of emotional means in the interest of the party's political goals. Style and subject matter of this art are actually described as "socialist-realist party art."

But any art form that to the bureaucrats seems abstract and not understandable, or is even critical of the system or some of its characteristics, or appeals to human conscience against social injustice and suppression, this kind of avant-garde and disturbing art is not accepted by bureaucratic regimes, but persecuted and prohibited.[30] The approach to art is totally utilitarian with the result that all art forms and all artists are pressed into this kind of politically subservient position by means of an openly disciplinarian, dictating, and censoring control by the party apparatus and the subordinated state cultural associations.

However, this is not to say that there are no works of art at all forthcoming in these countries. Besides the unmistakable party conformist trash that has very little in common with real art, there are literary works, paintings, sculptures, and movies presenting certain artistic values but they are limited to subject matters that do not comment on social conditions. The artists have to deal with petty or even trivial problems of human life, or they have to settle for neutral subject matters, the alternatives being either to go along and glorify reality, or to risk falling victim to the party censorship for expressing social criticism through their works.[31]

Well-known artists, scientists, athletes, and other personalities of "public value" who are not interested in politics and avoid commenting on controversial political issues but become nationally and internationally known on the basis of their achievements are pampered by the party bureaucracy and offered the best material working conditions possible. These personalities make their countries popular throughout the world without threatening the system since they adopt an apolitical stand, and they are propagandistically exhibited and exploited by the party bureaucracy, especially if they are not party members. In any case, the party prefers these personalities by far to the party-member artists who critically examine and question, or propose to reform, the system. While nonparty, apolitical, or conformist artists enjoy innumerable privileges, the oppositional artists have to suffer the meanest harassment and persecution.

Under the present materially backward and politically restricted conditions, financial benefits, foreign travel (especially to Western countries), and public distinction obviously provide strong incentives for young people. These allow them to reach material and social positions to which they otherwise would not have had access, particularly as nonparty members. This together with concentrated state aid and support explains the relatively spectacular achievements by the Eastern European countries in the area of sports, to give just one example.

The cultural associations provide the party apparatus with a decisive power over the artists for three reasons: first, in the socialist system artists are financially dependent on state aid distributed through the cultural associations; second, without the authorization of these associations they cannot exhibit, publish, and sell; third, without the agreement of the cultural associations they cannot even officially call themselves artists and can therefore be harassed by the police for "inactivity" and "vagrancy." In order to control the activities of these people, the party fills the important positions within the cultural associations—which officially are reporting to the Ministry of Culture—with activists who are loyal to the party but mostly second-rate artists. As a result, many artistic works of outstanding quality are suppressed or destroyed.[32]

And yet, despite this huge machinery of misinformation, unscientific and demagogic propaganda, and a "cultural education" supervised and controlled by specific state organs and by the party apparatus, there are still articles, reports, books, and works of art that manage to truthfully describe, uncover, or fight the real situation. This proves that even the most totalitarian regime is incapable of reducing to complete silence an element such as human conscience, that it is incapable of preventing those internal "explosions" that keep erupting because of an individual decision by a member of the scientific, artistic, or publishing community to tell the truth to the people. This kind of intellectual resistance is on the increase in the communist countries, varying in extent and intensity from one country to the next. But it is certainly remarkable that even a system based on the absolutistic moral principle of "socialism," which grants in advance an almost theocratic pardon for every deed done in the name of socialism, cannot suppress people's consciences. It is equally remarkable that despite all the odds there are always intelligent people with strong emotional ties and a deep feeling of commitment to the people who are willing to fight desperately for truth and its recognition.

NOTES

1. Chapter II, Section 4 of the Constitution of the CSSR declares: "The leading force in society and in the state is the avantgarde of the working class, the Communist Party of Czechoslovakia, the voluntary fighting union of the most active and conscious citizens from the ranks of the workers, peasants, and the intelligentsia."

2. For simplicity's sake I will use the term "Politburo," although the different Communist Parties use different names for this organ.

3. Shortly before his death, at a private party on his seventieth birthday, Novotny himself said in a moment of self-criticism "that he did not have the intellectual background for his position, but that he had been too conceited to admit this fact." *Listy*, no. 6 (August 1975), p. 4.

4. Number of positions approved by:

CC-CPC	541
Politburo of the CC-CPC	837
Secretariat of the CC-CPC	2499
Sections of the CC-CPC	5059

From the records of the Fourteenth Party Congress of the CPC, Prague 1968, p. 25. The Moscow Declaration did not recognize this so-called "illegal" party congress of the CPC, which took place August 22-27, 1968.

5. Ibid., p. 24.

6. Ibid., p. 38.

7. Khrushchev at the Twentieth Party Congress, Moscow, February 25, 1956.

8. N. V. Podgorny, in *Pravda*, June 13, 1975.

9. According to *Izvestia* of January 19, 1975, agricultural machinery was actually operating during only 48 percent of the entire working time, while for the rest of the time it sat unproductively, waiting for repairs or skilled operators.

10. See also Khrushchev, ibid., and J. Pelikan, ed. *Das unterdrueckte Dossier* [The suppressed file] (Vienna, 1970), p. 67.

11. Khrushchev, ibid.

12. Data on political trials and political prisoners in the Eastern European countries are hardly available. However, the International Committee for the Defense of Human Rights in the USSR has collected important material on today's Soviet concentration camps in a report published in Brussels, February 26, 1973, pp. 3-9. See also J. Pelikan, *Sozialistische Opposition in der CSSR* [Socialist opposition in the CSSR] (Cologne, 1974).

13. Between 1968 and 1970, the Czech Communist Party lost 600,000 out of its 1,600,000 members, who either left the party, were excluded, or had their membership annulled. In Bohemia and Moravia, the number totalled 550,000, or 42 percent of the Bohemian-Moravian party membership. About half of the members had joined the party before World War II, during the German occupation, or before the communist seizure of power in 1948. Out of 25,000 original members having joined the CPC before the war, only 8,000 had remained in the party. Out of the 500 still living members of the international brigades who had fought in the Spanish Civil War, only 30 still belonged to the party.

14. In May 1975, the well-known Czech philosopher Karel Kosik wrote in a letter to his French colleague Jean-Paul Sartre: "I really exist in two ways. I do not exist, and still I exist. I am dead—but I am alive. . . ." *Listy*, no. 5 (July 1975), p. 30.

15. In the CSSR, a long list of names of the people excluded from the party was secretly distributed to all colleges and universities, which were forbidden to enroll children of listed families. In addition, general guidelines for college admissions became more restrictive, establishing priorities in the following order:

1. students, members of the CPC
2. children from families with both parents being members of the CPC
3. children from politically active families
4. children from worker and peasant families
5. children from families with one parent being a member of the CPC
6. others.

16. A. Dubček, letter to the National Assembly of the Federation and to the Slovak National Council, October 28, 1974, *Listy*, no. 3 (April 1975).

17. "For fear of losing his job, a teacher teaches things in school which he doesn't believe in himself. Fearful about his future, a student repeats these teachings. For fear not to be allowed to continue his studies, a youngster joins the youth organization and does everything he is told to do. For fear that his son or daughter will not collect enough points to qualify for admission to a school according to a monstrous political grading system, a father takes on various duties and "volunteers" to do everything he is asked to do. For fear of possible consequences, people participate in elections, vote for the official candidates, and pretend to believe that this ritual is a genuine election process. Fearful about their existence, positions, or careers, people attend meetings, vote for everything they are told to vote for. At the most, they keep silent. Afraid, they make humiliating declarations of self-criticism and repentance, and fill in innumerable humiliating questionnaires. Afraid to be denounced, they do not dare voice their real opinions publicly, and often not even privately. . . . For the same reason, they participate in official festivities, manifestations, and parades. For fear of being out of work many scientists and artists profess ideas which they don't really believe in, write lies, join official organizations, and participate in activities they know to be worthless. They even mutilate or deform their own work. In order to save themselves, some people even report others for activities in which they themselves have participated. . . ." V. Havel, letter in *Listy*, no. 5 (July 1975), p. 32.

18. Doesn't this remind us of the Inquisition during the Middle Ages? See H. C. Lea, *Geschichte der Spanischen Inquisition* [History of the Spanish Inquisition] (Leipzig, 1912), III:119.

19. In the CSSR, for example, members of the Politburo and a few chosen ministers have the exclusive access and use of a huge reservation in one of the most beautiful parts of the country, offering the most modern housing and recreation facilities. It was here, under conditions of greatest affluence, that Novotny came up with the slogan "Our generation will live to see Communism" (the second phase, the phase of affluence, as opposed to the first, the socialist phase).

20. For years, Novotny had distributed to the members of the Politburo monthly sums of money that exceeded their normal salary. When this practice came to light during the months of the "Prague Spring," the most conservative and dogmatic among the members of the Central Committee of the CPC were the most upset, not because of what had happened but because they had not been included in this privilege.

21. "... These gentlemen only talk about their love for manual work, but they dread it more than anything. They brag about their working-class origins but none of them ever returns to working in the factory. They are capable of any villainy, but nobody will make them go back to the factory or the field, not voluntarily...." J. Putik, *Brana blazenych* [The gate of the blessed] (Prague, 1969), p. 52.

22. From the ranks of these communists emerged all those groups that were the first to recognize that the socialist system in the USSR had degenerated into a bureaucratic system, and that attempted to break Stalin's power in order to reverse the development. They were liquidated by the Stalinist bureaucrats as "Trotskyite traitors" and "Bukharinite petty-bourgeois opportunists." The same kind of communists founded the Petoefi Circle in Hungary, aiming at a liberalization of the system. From a similar background came the Polish and, finally, the Czech reformers who fought for a democratization and humanization of the system. Although differing in political maturity and in their understanding of the causes of communist degeneration, they all were convinced of the necessity of fighting the bureaucratization of party and society in the interest of their people.

23. Statistics published by the Prague City Party Committee show that on June 30, 1973, only 13 percent of the members in Prague (most industrialized region of the CSSR) were workers. This is even less than the relatively low statewide percentage of 17 percent ... and this despite all the promises by the Fourteenth Party Congress to do everything possible in order to increase membership among the workers.

24. The situation is very different in the various communist countries. In the CSSR, for example, the party apparatus today has hardly any ideological influence on the majority of the population outside the party membership. In the GDR and the USSR, this influence is possibly stronger for specific historical and other reasons. While less strong in Poland and Hungary, this influence has strong nationalistic overtones in Rumania.

25. After Husak had come to power, agents of the state police (Documentation Section of the State Police), for example, received 5000. Kč for editing a pamphlet of a few pages (about 15 minutes radio time) slandering the leading Czech reformers. This sum equals two and a half months' pay of a qualified worker in the CSSR.

26. See more on this subject in Ota Šik, *The Third Way—Marxist-Leninist Theory and Modern Industrial Society* (London-New York, 1976).

27. The public in the West knows very little about the real situation, since it is beneath the dignity of most Western newspapers, journals, and publishers to translate such humbug. One of the few exceptions is the publication by Damnitz Verlag of J. Hajek, *"Demokratisierung oder Demontage"* (Munich, 1969). The opportunistic party ideologist and responsible editor of the party journal *Tvorba* gives a completely

one-sided and biased account of the development of the so-called "revisionists" and "counterrevolutionaries" in the CSSR. It would fill several volumes to repeat all the lies contained in this book. But one fact has to be mentioned. According to Hajek, O. Šik as director of the Reform Commission under the Novotny regime at first "was against workers' councils in the enterprises" and only during the Spring months "suddenly changed his attitude." Hajek intentionally does not mention the fact that under pressure from the Politburo, the entire reform proposal had to be completely revised six times, and that above all the proposals concerning democratization in the enterprises had to be eliminated. Many even more harmless proposals than the feared workers' councils had to be omitted. It was only due to the relentless and skillful efforts of the entire reform commission that any reforms were implemented at all. . . . The reformers had to fight the bureaucracy's resistance every step of the way. As late as June 1968, a proposal concerning the general introduction of workers' councils was rejected twice by the majority of the ministers (who had been members of the Novotny government). Under these circumstances I had no other choice than to address myself directly to the public in order to get this proposal accepted. Why doesn't Hajek mention this, and why doesn't he go on fighting for the workers' councils since he considers them to be in the workers' interests?

28. "Do you accept that the dogma taught by the Church is the only truth, that there is no other truth besides or beyond this truth? . . . Whoever wants to serve the faith has to surrender to the principles laid down by the faith, without hesitating, without questioning, without doubting, without a shadow of second thoughts, and with unlimited trust in the authorities." From A. Andrzejewski, *Finsternis bedeckt die Erde* [Darkness covers the earth] (Munich, 1961), pp. 48, 55. Who wants to claim that inquisitorial demands of faith belong only to the Middle Ages?

29. During the purges in the CSSR in the early 1970s, thousands among the most capable scientists, professors, and teachers were dismissed from schools and research institutes and forced to give up their scientific work and teaching activities. Those allowed to stay on had to fill in humiliating questionnaires, sign condemnations of the revisionists, and address notes of thanks to the Soviet liberators. Not only teachers excluded from the party are forbidden to teach, but also their spouses who continue to live with them. The social sciences in the universities were completely "reversed." During the 1971-72 term, 13 disciplines could not be taught at the Philosophical Faculty of Karls University, among others philosophy, sociology, Oriental studies, ethnography, musicology, art history. The Political Science Institute of the Academy of Sciences, and the Institute of Political Sciences of the Philosophical Faculty were closed. Among the historical disciplines the history of the twentieth century was the hardest hit. Economics suffered enormously, with many of the most outstanding economists dismissed, and teaching brought back to the level of the 1950s. Equally reduced were the departments of law, sociology, literature, Slavic and German studies, and so forth.

30. See also A. I. Solzhenitsyn, letter to the Fourth All-Union Congress of Soviet Writers, "On the Responsibility of the Writer."

31. V. Havel, letter in "Listy," no. 5 (July 1975), p. 37.

32. Ibid.

4
BUREAUCRATIC ANTIDEMOCRATISM

ANTIDEMOCRATIC ARGUMENTATION

The practically unlimited power of the bureaucratic apparatus can be secured only by repression of the people's democratic liberties. This means that there is no freedom of speech, assembly, and association, no right to free elections and divestment of political representatives. There is no "fuller democracy due to less formalities and simplification of elections and divestments," which in 1918 Lenin still saw as the ideal. Also, there can be no question of closer ties between the people and the production and management units, or of an election of workers' councils in the enterprises as demanded by Lenin at the time. The people have far fewer liberties than in the despised bourgeois democracies, and consequently there is not only no "possibility of eliminating the bureaucracy and making do without it" and not even the "hint of a possibility,"[1] but the bureaucracy has become the absolute master of the people. By eliminating the internal as well as the external antibureaucratic factors under conditions where the bureaucracy is no longer controlled by any private owners of means of production, the *bureaucracy has become the absolute power*. Instead of a dictatorship of the proletariat, the total dictatorship of the bureaucracy has evolved.

The party bureaucracy is fully aware of the fact that in order to maintain its privileged position within society as well as its unlimited and absolute power, it cannot afford to grant any democratic liberties. Although the system needs effective economic development, it is not in the bureaucracy's interest to achieve this goal by granting real autonomy to economic enterprises, by introducing a socialist-free market order, and by democratizing macro-planning. But even more than the resulting decline of its economic power,[2] the party bureaucracy fears democratic freedom for the people since such a development would not only imply a restriction of bureaucratic power but lead to an independent evolution of democracy, to the self-government of the people in the largest sense of the word, and thus to an end of bureaucratic rule.

The specifically economic and political interests of the party bureaucracy that result from its superior and remote position and motivate its entire activity also have a decisive impact on its ideological thinking. The major role of the official party ideology is to justify the continuity of the bureaucratic system. In accordance with this goal, any request for democratic liberties has to be interpreted as a "bourgeois request aiming at the restoration of capitalism." At the same time, the current bureaucratic system has to be advertised as the system "which best represents the interests of the working class and therefore is the least formal and the broadest form of democracy."[3]

However, the entire ideological literature of the Eastern European countries does not contain one single analysis of the political institutions, relationships, and mechanisms in socialism which would prove that there are truly democratic rights of the working class, that there is free political activity outside of the party apparatus and independent of its authorization.

Instead of offering concrete analyses of the actual situation, the official "theory" and propaganda deliver nothing but quotes from the "classics" and abstract contentions in the line of "it has to be the way Lenin said, and that is the way it is." There is no evidence, no explanation, no confrontation with reality. Although the necessity of "analytical works" is discussed, the official ideologues avoid getting down to a serious theoretical analysis of existing relationships and their internal contradictions, for the uncovering of objective contradictions inherent in socialist society, as well as of contradictions existing between abstract theory and practical reality, would not be to the advantage of the ruling elite.

After the repression of the progressive reform movement in Czechoslovakia, the country saw its bureaucratic system reinstalled and reinforced. Ideological attacks against the reformers are designed to wipe out their influence on the people. However, even this all-out ideological campaign is not able to counter the reformers' concrete analysis, evidence, and argumentation with anything but the old abstract "classical" doctrines and the well-known arsenal of name-calling. Commonplace references to the "class-conscious approach of the issue of democracy" are intended to present the striving of the reformers for a democratic socialism as "non-Marxist" and "antiworking class." The leading figure in this campaign was G. Husak, who exploited the issue as a means of consolidating his own position by securing the party apparatus' support. In order to illustrate Husak's bureaucratic-propagandistic methods it may be useful to include here the unabbreviated version of his argumentation on the subject of socialist democracy:

> While working on the basic issues of the socialist state Lenin also turned his attention to the question of socialist democracy. V. I. Lenin examined the abstract considerations concerning democracy, and the issue of democracy in general, with merciless criticism. In his work "The Proletarian Revolution and the Renegate Kautsky" he said the following on the subject of pure democracy: "By the way, 'pure democracy' is not only a cliche used by ignorants proving their lack of understanding of the class struggle and of the nature of the state. It is also a triple empty cliche because in communist society democracy, by changing and becoming a habit, will 'wither away' but never evolve into 'pure democracy.'"
>
> As in the case of liberties, humanism, etc., the issue of democracy, its forms and future development always have to be viewed in the context of concrete economic, political, social, and international realities at the given level of socialist construction. Furthermore, the class-conscious approach to a number of issues has to be taken into account: Democracy for whom, for what, to which extent, and in relation to whom? Otherwise, we will just have abstract slogans on democracy without any real intent on democratic evolution but designed to cover up for totally different goals and interests, and to mislead the mass of the working classes. This is exactly what many of the new Marxist revisionists have in mind while advocating their theories on new socialist models. In this context it must be stressed that Lenin thought the problems of the state and of socialist democracy to be essential not only theoretically but in practical politics. This complex point of view has a double significance. Firstly, to help evaluate the activities of various right-wing opportunistic and revisionistic factions and their abuse of democratic concepts. Theoretically, and in a similar way as Kautsky and others during Lenin's time, these factions recognize, at least temporarily, many of the principal tenets of Marxist-Leninist theory on democracy. However, from a practical political standpoint, from the standpoint of concrete conclusions, tasks and measures, the new revisionists forget all about these doctrines. These are the forgotten truths of Marxism which Lenin had mentioned on several occasions and which many of the advocates of a new socialist model forgot in the CSSR in 1968. But the

very extent to which theoretical and political-practical concepts of state and democracy are harmonized in the policy of the party, or rather, to which extent they are forgotten, separates the Marxist-Leninist from the revisionists and opportunists.

Secondly, Lenin's theoretical concept of a socialist democracy was essentially linked to political-practical considerations concerning the soviets (councils), their functions and tasks. On the basis of analysis and comparison of Marx's and Engel's opinions on the democratic traits of the Paris Commune with the democracy of soviets, Lenin arrived at the conclusion that the proletarian democracy constitutes a higher form of democracy, a democracy for the great majority of the people, and that it represents a violent repression of the exploiters. Its new quality consists in the fact that it reaches beyond the limits of parliamentarianism—of the so-called representative democracy—and evolves into a democracy for the masses in the sense that the working classes become direct subjects of proletarian power, directly participating in the making and implementing of decisions.[4]

Let us forget about the bureaucratic-elaborate style that is so typical of the emptiness and unreality of "Leninist" propaganda, and let us instead concentrate on the allegations brought against the revisionists.

What motivates the fight against the "representatives of so-called pure democracy"? Who among the reformers demanded a "pure democracy"? The very concrete issue was "democracy for the people" in a society where for 20 years the regime had repressed free democratic expression of opinion of the working population, where almost 90 percent of the population had been reduced to political inequality and been excluded from active political life. Therefore, the very concrete issue was to answer Lenin's question of "democracy for whom," to establish conditions for a genuine democracy for the working classes, for the "fuller democracy due to fewer formalities and easier elections and divestments," which Lenin once proclaimed but never realized. The issue was to create conditions under which the "emphasis was shifted from the formally *recognized* liberties (as they exist in bourgeois parliamentary government systems) to the factual guarantee to the workers of *using* these liberties, for example, by replacing the *recognition* of the right to assembly by the actual *use* by the workers of the best meeting places; by replacing the recognition of free expression of opinion by the use of the best printing presses, etc."[5]

However, the fact that the state or, rather, the party apparatus decides on public meetings, the use of premises and of the press, as well as on any political action means that the people do not actually enjoy these liberties. This situation reflects complete submission to the ruling powers' opinion and interests, which obviously do not coincide with those of the population at large, since the ruling power cannot tolerate any real criticism and top-level personnel changes. A totalitarian regime is characterized by the fact that it only allows for conformist political activity; it is undemocratic because it does not allow for any political activity that may threaten the powerful position of the ruling personalities.

One of the most prominent demagogic features of the ruling power in the "socialist" states is exactly this: the leadership is personified in the socialist system. Any measures taken in the direction of democratization and aimed at implementing the possibility of controlling and dismissing of political functionaries, of *electing* representatives from the rank of the people, of voicing differences of opinion among political representatives were invariably viewed as bourgeois attacks against socialism. Not even within the Communist Parties could such democratic conditions be guaranteed, and invariably a communist striving to create such conditions would be accused of being an antisocialist element, which deserves elimination.

How is it possible to constantly invoke the "class-conscious" viewpoint when private ownership of means of production has been eliminated 20 years ago, or, in the case of the USSR, 50 years ago, the bourgeoisie having been liquidated? How could there be a real danger to the all-powerful socialist state in the presence of a few surviving members of these former classes that had always been limited in number? How could a small group of descendants of the formerly propertied classes possibly win the support of the large masses of workers? Is not the fear of the restoration of capitalism one of the most serious blames directed at bureaucratic "socialism"?

A social system cannot be called legitimate when after many decades it has not been able to win the voluntary support of the working population and as long as it is afraid of genuine democratization because such a process might be exploited by "procapitalist elements" fighting socialism. Actually, this kind of societal order openly admits to the fact that the working classes have to be repressed by the bureaucratic power and deprived of democratic freedom since under democratic conditions the representatives of bureaucratic socialism could not win in the competition with their capitalist counterparts.

This is a very real fear with all communists who are afraid of democracy, and this fear is more or less openly expressed by Husak. He stresses the fact that there are still members of the former bourgeoisie and petty bourgeoisie alive[6] today in Czechoslovakia, which for him is sufficient as an argument against a broadening of democratic rights for the working classes. How does he explain his fear that a small number of bourgeois "old men" may win over today's young workers? Have not the communists contended all along that the bourgeoisie had wielded power over some segments of the working population only because it controlled the decisive ideological instruments, the political parties, the state apparatus, on the basis of its economic wealth? Now that all these elements can be activated in favor of the communists are they afraid of a handful of former bourgeois politicians who have been deprived of all economic power? It should be added that in the USSR practically no members of the former ruling classes are left today.

In reality, the party bureaucracy is afraid of the workers and not of the remnants of the bourgeoisie and petty bourgeoisie. This fear dates all the way back to the Kronstadt uprising. If the working class were relatively happy with the "socialist" system, there would be no danger of it being won over by representatives of capitalism. In other words, the insignificant remnants of the capitalist class should not be a threat to a socialist state even if this state allowed for democratic freedom. In any case, the surviving former members of the bourgeoisie are all today ordinary workers, employees, or members of cooperatives (cooperative farmers or craftsmen)[7] who do not own any means of production or substantial wealth. They are certainly not in a position to exert any ideological influence on the population by means of mass media communication. If the communist bureaucrats are nevertheless afraid that such a small segment of the former bourgeoisie could under democratic conditions suddenly win a decisive influence over the working masses, then this amounts to a declaration of bankruptcy. It is indirectly being admitted that neither the "socialist" system nor the education dispensed over several decades—in other words, the propaganda—have been successful enough to ensure that the working class population would not become "fighters for the restoration of capitalism."

Furthermore, the argument that remnants of the bourgeoisie might receive financial support from the capitalist states for antisocialist political activities actually translates into a serious accusation against the politics and ideology of the current ruling groups in the "socialist" countries. Not only could the "socialist" state easily discover and cut off any substantial foreign financial aid in support of antistate activities, but even if this kind of aid could somehow be materialized, the long-ruling "socialist" power would still be able to provide substantially larger financial means for propaganda purposes. When Lenin mentioned the momentarily greater powers of the bourgeoisie in relation to the revolutionary government, he stressed the fact that this situation was only typical of the initial phase in the evolution of socialism. After decades of "socialist" rule in all of today's "socialist states," such an argument cannot be introduced seriously any more.[8]

GENERALIZATION OF INTERESTS

What does Husak mean when he says that "pure democracy" does not exist and that this fact has to be taken into account in both theory and practice? Obviously, a democratic system can never expect to satisfy the interests of everybody as long as contradictory and mutually exclusive interests do exist within a society. This will always be true in a socialist society as well, where the means of production no longer are the private property of a minority and where everyone except the handicapped has to live from the income of his labor. Though capitalist interests no longer represent economically and politically powerful interests, a generalized interest has to be enforced, the interests of a majority overruling the interests of a minority. It is virtually excluded that all members of society have at any time totally identical interests and goals. It will always be up to a majority to decide on a society's development. However, the point is to establish which is the genuine interest of the majority by giving this majority interest the opportunity to evolve from the confrontation of differing interests and to manifest itself in the form of a compromise as the generalized interest of the majority of the people.

In the case of a state that has eliminated capitalism several decades ago, it is erroneous to maintain that only a Communist Party would be able to recognize and promote the general interest of the working people while at the same time keeping capitalist, anti-worker interests from taking over. This conception is erroneous for the following two reasons.

First, *it simplifies the process of generalization of greatly differing interests representing large segments of the population.* Any future development of a socialist societal entity is possible and conceivable in various concrete alternatives. Even when an evolution toward a so-called "higher communist affluent society" is anticipated, this is such a general and vague image of the future that the concrete development over the next 10 to 20 years can occur in an infinite number of variants. An all-deciding grouping of individuals cannot possibly recognize and express all variants, not to mention select and realize the one and only right solution.[9] We can talk of a democratic generalization of differing interests and the formulation of a majority interest only in a system where the citizens freely formulate and publish different models of development and proposals for all spheres of societal activity, where they can win others over to their point of view and set up organizations, where the different groupings have the possibility of discussing their ideas, of adapting to, and agreeing with, each other.

Second, *it overlooks the specific interest of the bureaucracy as opposed to the interests of society at large.* In the striving for abstract communist ideals ("technical revolution," "affluence of consumer products," "everybody works according to his capacity—everybody receives according to his needs," and so forth), the bureaucracy may share the same interests with the people ("Who would reject such goals?"). But when it comes to implementing concrete political and economic measures for the next few weeks, months, or years, the bureaucracy will always oppose any proposals and plans that might restrict or curtail its own position of power, control, cadre selection, organizational plans, financial distribution, growth regulation, and so forth. The fact that specific interests of the bureaucratic apparatus, and particularly of the powerful party apparatus, do exist within a one-party system and that these interests are in permanent opposition to the interests of the rest of the population totally excludes the possibility that this same apparatus determines the actual societal development in accordance with the general interests of the people.

The inevitable contradiction existing between the people's general interests and the bureaucracy's specific power interests can be demonstrated by countless examples. There is virtually no bureaucratic decision that does not translate the bureaucracy's specific interests as more or less opposed to the interests of the people. When in the CSSR a decision has to be taken on the allocation of paper that is in short supply, the official party organ *Rude Pravo* gets the largest supply of paper although this newspaper has the highest quota of unsold copies. Other more interesting and more widely read papers, however, are granted only a very limited supply of paper. Or, when there is a choice between two candidates for the position of director general in a large enterprise—one a highly qualified expert who, although a party member, once had opposed in a meeting a certain proposal submitted by the county secretary; the other, a less qualified person but who for many years had been used by the county secretariat as a speaker at party meetings—the party organ most certainly will choose the latter of the two candidates. These examples make it quite obvious that each decision, no matter how unimportant or how far-reaching, should be questioned, because under different conditions such as the existence of alternatives and the nonexistence of a monopolistic bureaucratic power, the generalization of interests and the expression of a will would be arrived at by a totally different process and become manifest in distinctly different decisions.

Therefore, the communist argument used to assert the necessity of the leading role of the party is nothing more than a propaganda slogan that "freedom is the recognized necessity," that "only the Communist Party is able to recognize and predict the objectively essential societal development on the basis of the Marxist-Leninist theory," which implies "to enable the people by its leadership to act freely." As far as there are any recognizable objective patterns of development in society, they can only be theoretically expressed by total abstraction as very basic and long-term historical tendencies. Such long-term historical patterns will always emerge from a variety of unexpected processes and events that shape the actual type of societal development.[10]

This is true also in the case of the socialist society, for the so-called conscious application of the known laws of development means, at best, nothing but respecting various basic interactions. Thus, for example, the development of productive forces initiates numerous changes in production, in the division of labor and distribution of products, and so forth, which, in turn, have an influence on the changes in productive forces. However, in which way does this fact help predict the development of productive forces over the next five years? Or, how relevant is the "law of regular, proportional development" to the concrete production structure during these five years and to the proportionate production of different goods? There are many concrete alternatives as to the future production development. Although more or less determined by past developments, these alternatives nevertheless are reflections of man's free will.[11]

Also, the great number of freely chosen models for future development that can all be expressions of a profound objective necessity is still only an abstraction, for the actual development depends in all its aspects on innumerable and unpredictable elements that are likely to appear in many variations. There is, therefore, no reason why one single party should decide which concrete form the economic, political, and cultural development is to take, since even the shaping of the future economy presupposes a certain margin of free decision. If, in addition, this one party is actually being manipulated by a party bureaucracy that uses the decision-making process for promoting its own specific power interests, its decisions will only reflect the "freedom of the bureaucrats." Such a claim to decision making cannot be justified by commonplaces on the "recognized necessity," and the like. On the contrary, whenever people decide on certain basic issues intended essentially to shape their future, the majority should be able to assert itself and reflect the result of a real confrontation and generalization of interests arrived at among the different segments and groups within the society of a socialist state.

The very concept of socialist democracy is simplified and falsified by all those who do not acknowledge the existence of a broad range of differing interests even within a socialist society, and who do not conceive of the necessity of pluralistic groupings of interests and opinions as a condition for a genuinely democratic generalization of interests, for the expression of majority interests, and as one of the essential factors in counteracting a bureaucratic hegemony. Not even the most vigorous assertion that the Soviet dictatorship of the proletariat is the "broadest democracy for the people" can change reality. And reality is this: the people are not allowed to express their opinion on interests presented by the bureaucracy as "the people's interests," the people have no means of changing bureaucratic decisions, and, because of a lack of objective information, are not even in a position to judge what their real interests may be.

If the communist bureaucracy were genuinely convinced that the majority of its past decisions, measures, and procedures always corresponded to the interests of the working population, it would not have to fear an authentic democratization process. On the contrary, under liberal conditions it should be doing particularly well when competing against political groupings and movements that try to promote capitalist—and therefore "antagonistic"—interests foreign to the working classes. If nevertheless there is in the "socialist" countries such great fear of capitalist restoration, this can only be explained by the fact that the bureaucrats rightly recognize that their political activity over several decades has failed to win the support of the largest segments of the population.

If, as Husak keeps implying, and Soviet ideologues readily confirm today,[12] it was really only the fear of free political movements giving former bourgeois parties' members a chance to impose a return to capitalism, the democratization process could be restricted by certain measures ensuring a definite ban on capitalist ownership of means of production. It should be sufficient to include basic laws into the constitution of a socialist country stipulating that, for instance, a means of production requiring an outside work force, or more than a couple of apprentices, may not be privately owned. This or a similar basic law was what the Czech reformers had in mind. Simultaneously, the country's constitution should only be modified on the basis of a direct referendum, with a required two-thirds or even three-quarters majority of the votes as an additional safeguard.[13]

Under such conditions, an overwhelming majority of the working population would have to favor the reintroduction of capitalism in order to bring about such a change. If at this point a bureaucratic ideologue should argue that the restorers of capitalism might step beyond legality and reestablish a capitalist economy by counterrevolutionary means, this kind of argument would disavow the essence of Marxist theory. It would imply that the "socialist" state built over decades of efforts, that the broad mass of the workers with their People's Militia, that the carefully organized, monopolistic Communist Party is afraid that some "bourgeois" party could suddenly muster such immense political and revolutionary forces as to be able to implement a basic modification of the system in defiance of all legal barriers. Did not the capitalist system, with the help of a constitution and its safeguard by the government, manage to resist for several decades organized anticapitalist and revolutionary forces attempting to disrupt its societal order?

What really happens here is that the ideologues of the "socialist" bureaucracy get entangled in contradictions while trying to justify the bureaucratic dictatorship with the alleged threat of a capitalist counterrevolution. On the one hand, they use as their main argument against a pluralistic socialist democracy the existence of the formerly petty-bourgeois classes and the harmful impact of their organizations and ideologies.[14] On the other hand, it is argued that the communists represent the strongest parties with the broadest support in the population. The same B. N. Topornin who elaborates on the great danger of the bourgeois and petty-bourgeois elements and takes this danger as justification for the "dictatorship of the proletariat," also says that "for the communists the idea of a political opposition in socialism is inacceptable not because they are afraid of competition as the enemies of Marxism want us to believe. In a socialist country, the Communist (workers') Party is the recognized leader of the working masses, a party that the workers accept as a deserving and undisputed authority. In all socialist countries, the communists have the party with the greatest membership, uniting the most active and conscious fighters for socialism from the ranks of the working classes and other segments of the working population. The Communist Party's position is firmly established within the socialist society as long as its organization and activity reflect Lenin's immortal principles of the new type of proletarian party."[15]

If the Communist Parties enjoy such an "indisputable authority with the workers" why don't they give them the opportunity to freely discuss, travel, inform themselves, set up organizations, and vote? Communist authority should even increase if under democratic conditions their parties gained the support of the majority by means of better ideas, better political goals, and activities. If it is true that "the communists cannot accept an opposition because an opposition would lack social roots and support from this or that class,"[16] then it is even less understandable that they are afraid of allowing for pluralistic-democratic conditions.

In reality, though, all this is empty propaganda. Topornin's book is typical of the kind of works written without scientific method but which earn their authors the desired recognition of the party bureaucracy. This book, whose subject is the political system of socialism, does not mention with one single word the bureaucracy, its role, interests, and activities, although Lenin himself shortly before his death had perceived the potential danger arising from the bureaucratization of the system and of the party. Indeed, from its position of increasing power, the very bureaucracy "rightfully" rejects democracy because it fears the people's accumulated anger and because it knows that under democratic conditions it would forfeit its monopolistic position. For this very reason, the bureaucracies of Czechoslovakia's neighboring countries have united to help repress the dangerously contagious Czech reform movement.

FEAR OF ANTIBUREAUCRATIC DEMOCRATIZATION

In reality, though, it was not fear of the Czechoslovakian bourgeoisie and counterrevolution that led to the violent intervention in the CSSR but fear of democratic freedom for the Czechoslovakian people. Not Czech socialism but its state-monopolistic and bureaucratic parody was endangered. Here again, as several times before, the initiative came from progressively minded communists who had become aware of the perverted contents of this kind of "socialism" and who had sensed a general popular disgust with the system. These communists decided to act when they became conscious of the contradiction and weakness inherent in the system, when they understood that repression, corruption, and deceitful propaganda cannot be the elements with which to build a socialist society, and that a genuinely socialist order can only be ensured by an authentic and timely democratization process on the basis of a constitutionally guaranteed socialist ownership system. Never before had the Czechoslovakian communists enjoyed such broad and enthusiastic support in the population; never before was there a greater chance of modifying the integral characteristics of the system in view of establishing for the first time a democratic and humanitarian form of socialism.

The reformers had carefully researched their proposals for

essential societal modifications. One of their major goals was the introduction of specific *internal and external antibureaucratic factors* in order to restrict the horrifying growth of bureaucratization and to break the bureaucracy's hegemonistic rule.

Proposals for economic reform were based on the perception that the overall complex optimality of production development in socialist enterprises cannot be ensured by a central planning and control mechanism and that only real market pressure would be able to effectively counteract the bureaucratization of production management. The innovative combination of a socialist, regulated market involving collectively owned enterprises with a program of basic guidelines at the macroeconomic level would not only have resulted in a certain degree of antibureaucratic independence and responsibility of the enterprise collectives, but also would have stimulated a genuine interest by the enterprises themselves in reaching optimal production decisions designed to meet social requirements. At the same time, however, overall planning and market regulation were expected to avoid a specifically capitalist market development as well as to forestall monopolistic income biases and consumption manipulation, cyclical crises, and inflation.

This kind of specifically socialist market relations acting as an antibureaucratic factor in the economic sector would have averted a bureaucratization of the administration of the economy by stimulating the workers' economic interests.

The democratization of planning at the macroeconomic level would have removed the task of establishing society's essential ideals and goals, as well as the related macroeconomic consumption and distribution pattern, from the hands of irresponsible, anonymous bureaucrats and delegated this responsibility to elected representatives of the people's major interests groups.

An overall democratization in politics, economy, and culture would have implied that any administrative and executive activity requiring professionally trained civil servants and managers is supervised by organs that from the lowest level through the highest ranks are exclusively composed of elected representatives of the people. All vital and essential decisions were to be made by representatives of the people elected for a definite term and removable at any time. Professional politicians were to be excluded from these elections. The population was to have the opportunity to associate in groupings on a short- or long-term basis in order to bring about modifications in one or the other sector of society. Organizations with a substantial membership—not only political parties but also the unions, farmers' associations, the large cultural associations, youth organizations, and so forth—that had demonstrated their willingness to support the constitution of a democratic society were to form a broad national front as its political basis. A political majority emerging from democratic elections would have decided on the concrete nature of a socialist development and incorporated the basically agreeable principles of the new societal order into the framework of its constitution. However, there was to be room for activities by other political groups that happened to be minorities. Groups aiming at a revision of the constitution would have to secure a legally determined minimum number of votes in order to request a referendum. Similarly, a legally determined percentage of votes would have to be required in view of the revision of a basic law.

This kind of democratization would have excluded from the onset any opportunity for some monopolistic bureaucratic apparatus, say, of a single political party, a military organization, or any other powerful organism, to force its absolute will on the population by filling important positions (cadre manipulation), by applying pressure, or by using corruption and ideological monopolization. Even in a formal system of soviets where the workers can elect their representatives at various levels but where there is only one monopolistic political apparatus controlling from backstage all activities that the unorganized mass of the people is unable to cope with on its own, the bureaucratic apparatus will inevitably evolve into the all-powerful ruling elite in charge of drafting modification proposals, regulations, laws, and cadre selection. Faced by this organized power, the individual is helpless and realizes only too late that he has been manipulated into accepting decisions that do not reflect his real interests but may even have a definitely negative impact.

The individual can learn to make the right choice among different development options only if he gets help and support from several competing political apparatus, from the information media, research institutions, and so forth that are no longer directly or indirectly dependent on capitalist owners, and if he is no longer manipulated by politicians who have arrived at a powerful position after many years of political activity and through innumerable contacts. He will learn to give his vote only to those delegates who will effectively represent his interests within the elected governing body. If each delegate can be elected only to a maximum of two terms and then returns to his previous occupation instead of changing one political job for another,[17] the accumulation of political power will become impossible. Thus, the people's representative does not turn into a political careerist acting in the interest of some powerful apparatus.

The reform movement in the CSSR was neither antisocialist, nor utopian. It had been theoretically prepared over many years and was fully backed by the Czech people. It would have broken the monopolistic power of the bureaucratic apparatus by cutting down its size and by subordinating it to the people's elected organisms. The election of people's representatives among candidates from political groups with differing platforms, reform proposals, and ultimate goals would have prevented any specific political group from controlling financial, organizational, or ideological means not available to the other groups. In addition, it would have made impossible the manipulation of majorities by monopolistic minorities. The combination of macroeconomic planning (choice of a five-year plan among two or three alternatives) with the election of political organs for a five-year term would have introduced a further element of objectivity into politics. Election campaigns would no longer have been dominated by political demagoguery designed to promote political careers but by discussions on the advantages and disadvantages of alternative solutions. A system of personnel rotation in all political institutions was to forestall the accumulation of power by a few individuals (a maximum of two terms in political positions), as well as to guarantee continuity within the organs (only part of the staff to be involved in the changeover after each term).

These were the basic features of the *antibureaucratic program* submitted by the Czechoslovakian reformers, and the very reason why the country was brought down by the united bureaucratic power under the pretext of "safeguarding socialism." In the West, there are still enough naive "revolutionaries" who prefer to believe in slogans such as "dictatorship of the proletariat" and "petty-bourgeois counterrevolution" to accepting criticism of the bureaucratic nature of the Soviet communist system. Many of these people are convinced that bureaucratism is the price to pay for living under socialism instead of capitalism. They are even willing to ignore repression, terror, and mass liquidation provided it is done in the interest of "socialism." However, these people diligently overlook the fact that the bureaucratic system has nothing in common with socialism, a fact which the majority of the workers living under this system are only too painfully aware of.

NOTES

1. See Chapter 2, note 27.
2. In an emergency, if the serious economic situation threatens to end its powerful position, the bureaucracy would probably have to give up its unlimited economic power in order to safeguard its political power.
3. "In contrast to the bourgeois societal orders, the Soviet Union has not only formally proclaimed the democratic liberties of its citizens but has also provided for

their practical implementation." Andropov, Election Speech, June 1975, quoted from "Neue Zuercher Zeitung," June 11, 1975; "The dictatorship of the proletariat means genuine democracy for the workers. It is an incomparably fuller democracy than that of the best among the prototypes of bourgeois political order." B. N. Topornin, *Das politische System des Sozialismus* [The political system of socialism] (Berlin, 1974); L. Brezhnev, "Life in our society is really democratic in all its aspects." *Pravda*, October 13, 1974.

4. G. Husak, "The Actuality of Lenin's Theories on the State and Democracy." Article written for *Pravda* on the 100th anniversary of Lenin's birthday, and published in *Rude Pravo* on April 16, 1970.

5. V. I. Lenin, "Extraordinary Seventh Party Congress of the CPR," *Collected Works*.

6. Husak, ibid.

7. In 1973, 88.3 percent of the population of the CSSR were workers and employees, and 10.6 percent were members of cooperatives. In Hungary, the relation was 82 percent to 13 percent; in Bulgaria, 59.6 percent to 39.2 percent, and in Rumania, 52.3 percent to 40.7 percent.

8. Whenever a bourgeois idea became popular in the "socialist" countries, the reason was not a bourgeois power basis within the country or pressure from abroad. It was always the result of the harmful and wrong politics of the existing power in these countries and of their unconvincing and false ideological activity. Communist politicians have always underestimated the intellectual level and the good judgment of their people.

9. A. Pelinka, *Dynamische Demokratie* [Dynamic democracy] (Stuttgart, 1974), p. 52.

10. F. Engels, letter to J. Bloch, September 21, 1890.

11. A. S. Mendelson, "The Plan in the Transition Period," *Planovoje Chozjajstov*, no. 8 (Moscow, 1928).

12. Topornin, *Das Politische System des Sozialismus*, p. 177.

13. This would have its social-structural justification in the fact that under capitalism the great majority of the people did not have capitalist ownership of the means of production either. Therefore; they would very probably not have supported its reintroduction in a direct polling.

14. Topornin, *Das Politische System des Sozialismus*, p. 72.

15. Ibid., p. 201.

16. Ibid.

17. This was another proposal submitted by the Czech reformers.

5
THE PERVERSION OF SOCIALISM

BUREAUCRATIC DEVELOPMENT OF PRODUCTIVE FORCES

The Soviet system meets hardly any of the criteria formulated by Marx and Engels, on the basis of their analysis of capitalism, as being characteristic features of a new communist society. These criteria should be manifest in the very first, or lower, phase of communism, the phase known since Lenin as the "socialist phase," in order to mark the beginning of a new society destined to overcome the contradictions of capitalism.

As most prominent among these new societal features, Marx and Engels always mentioned a faster development of productive forces as the expression of the fundamental law of historical materialism whose acceptance is a condition to establishing the necessity of overcoming capitalist economy and replacing it by more progressive socialist-economic relations. Socialist economic relations, or production relations, were to ensure a faster and more effective development of productive forces, cut economic losses, increase the efficiency of potential production factors, promote technology, increase labor productivity, and, consequently, provide for a higher standard of living. This was to reflect above all a balance between the new economic relations and the requirements of the highly developed productive forces.

The economic system of the communist countries of Eastern Europe, however, is far from reflecting this fundamental feature. All analyses and comparative studies show that this system by no means has reached the level of production efficiency typical of the capitalist economies in the Western industrial countries. To any economist who has even vaguely studied the available comparative data, this conclusion is more than convincing despite considerable difficulties resulting not only from complex conversions and differing statistical approaches, but also and above all from systematic political cover-ups and biases.

The fact that new industrial enterprises are set up with the help of state-centralized financial means in a relatively short span of time does not say anything about the development of productive forces in an industrially advanced "socialist" country. Even in Western capitalist countries, industrialization requires a considerable amount of state aid, and the total control exerted by a communist state over all means of accumulation undoubtedly accelerates the process of industrialization. In this period of truly extensive growth, new enterprises are established at the expense of the existing agricultural and industrial enterprises that are drained of all profits and allowances for depreciation. As long as free labor is available, from the agricultural sector and the ranks of the housewives, the industrial infrastructure can be easily extended, possibly at a faster pace than industrialization could be brought about in an entirely capitalist system. However, as soon as these labor reserves are exhausted, such an extensive industrial growth leads to considerable economic losses.[1]

The state-promoted accent on industrialization and especially on the growth of heavy industry[2] involves a continuous drain of labor away from other economic sectors (agriculture, transport, construction, trade, services, and so forth) and leads to major disproportions in economic development, thus resulting in a very negative impact on the people's standard of living. After decades of neglecting its agriculture, the Soviet Union changed from the once greatest grain-exporting country to a nation dependent on capitalist agriculture for its supply in grains. The totally backward construction sector caused such a housing shortage that even former highly industrialized Eastern European countries like the CSSR have fallen back to the level of developing countries.[3] The disproportionate expansion of heavy industry forced on the CSSR has resulted in a situation where the once export-intensive sectors of consumer-goods production have become totally outdated and inadequate, as in the case of shoes, textiles, glass, china, wood products, automobiles, and food.[4]

The system of command planning is not capable of securing a more intensive productivity growth based on fast technological change and appropriate modernization in existing enterprises. Insufficient replacement of existing production equipment, continued maintenance of technically outdated enterprises, and depreciated machinery describe the larger part of the production infrastructure. Since enterprises operate under the pressure of yearly increasing plans (planned production growth rate) while the allocated machinery and production equipment have hardly been technically improved to adapt to a faster pace of production, the only resource is to fight for the allocation of additional work force. This is the only means of attaining the prescribed production target in the individual enterprise, and it is the only way of maintaining a predominantly extensive growth of industrial production.

At the same time there is an unnatural, increasing demand for labor and investment in the industrial sector and especially in the field of heavy industry, a fact which clearly reflects the inefficiency of this kind of production development. Labor being concentrated in industry, there is an increasing shortage of work force in the other sectors of the economy. In addition, industrial production equipment is not used to capacity. As the number of workers in the second shift declines (since it is easier to hire labor for the first shift,) so does production capacity during the second shift. Under the pressure of production targets, an increasing number of enterprises even extend their capacities but without being granted additional work force, thus increasing the number of unfilled jobs and therefore of unused means of production.[5]

Also, this extensive growth leads to investment demands reflected in a threatening slowdown in capital accumulation. Together with the expansion of current assets (raw materials, semifinished products, energy, and so forth), growth investments constitute the so-called accumulation fund, a major part of the national income. If the accumulation fund increases at a faster rate than the national income, that is, if the percentage of the accumulation fund in the national income increases while labor increases at the same time, it is a clear sign of insufficient technological progress in production. The more production assets are needed for a determined growth rate in national income, and the more the percentage of accumulation assets in the national income (accumulation rate) has to increase in order to ensure growth of national income, the slower the rise of the people's living standard, which represents the other part of national income. The growing disparity between the increase in national income and the increase in accumulation assets[6] together with increasing demands on labor in industry is one of the major problems politicians in Eastern Europe have to face.[7]

Because, in any case, gross as well as net national product

(national income) per capita are lower in the Eastern European countries than in the Western industrial states and because due to the high accumulation rate the percentage of consumption in the gross national product as well as in the national income is smaller than in the West,[8] the precondition for the Eastern European countries to reach the Western level of per capita consumption is a substantial reduction of the accumulation rate and a faster growth rate of national income. The same is true for the average consumption of wage earners, which is substantially higher in the West than in the East.[9] However, this goal will be hard to achieve in view of decreasing capital productivity, especially since Western capital productivity is on the increase, or at least stable, as the long-term development of capital output ratios in most Western industrial countries seem to indicate.[10]

Insufficient technological development and lack of modernization in production, and the much-too-elevated percentage of labor in relation to production assets typical of the Eastern European countries are the most characteristic traits of a less-effective development of productive resources in the Soviet economic system as compared to Western industrial countries. It is not a coincidence that all Eastern European states, and especially the management of production enterprises, are strongly interested in importing technology and know-how from the West[11] despite relatively successful technological developments in the heavily subsidized armament industry. This is indeed the sector where the most substantial funds are invested and the best technologies applied (domestically developed as well as imported from the West), and where the most capable management and labor are concentrated. Exceptionally high wages in the defense industry create unusually strong incentives for faster and better research and development. Being a political priority sector, the defense industry benefits from such special advantages that its growth is not typical of the overall national production development. Also, expenditures are not budgeted in this sector of the economy, on the contrary, requirements are met no matter what the costs involved. There are no cost comparisons that might indicate that with greater efficiency and productivity production costs for politically required military products could be lowered by 20 or 30 percent, if not more.

Obviously, this must not be understood to mean that there are no technological improvements at all in the other production sectors. But since none of the monopolized enterprises operate under pressure to compete, let alone to sell, and since no high-level bureaucrat can assess the number and nature of innovations that the subordinate enterprise would be capable of introducing, the enterprise will operate accordingly. Since innovations always involve technical changes, job conversions, complicated supply operations resulting in loss of time and requiring greater personal dedication, which in turn tend to slow down the process of meeting the current plan's deadlines, an enterprise will try to avoid getting involved in too many innovative programs. There are always a few new products reported with great publicity to superior organs that in turn can "profitably sell" these achievements to higher-level political organizations. Many purely formal innovations involving hardly any extra time but not really representing any real progress either, are often made to justify higher prices for these so-called new products. Even a drop in quality can result in hidden price increases.[12] With the help of higher prices, an enterprise can more easily increase its production volume (pricewise) and thus report a fictitious increase in productivity.

Consequently, except in the area of propaganda, innovations remain quantitatively as well as qualitatively far behind the development in the West The advocates of absolute monopoly simply behave in the same way as Western companies would react if they no longer had to operate under market pressure and as, in fact, they begin to behave as soon as market pressure lets up and the monopolistic position is reinforced. In the West, however, this is still only an exceptional situation, and the absolute majority of enterprises has to remain competitive by pursuing research and development. For this very reason, the technology gap existing between the East and West does not narrow down but widens further at the disadvantage of the East. Consequently, productivity development, too, lags behind the productivity growth of the Western industrial countries.[13]

However, the uneconomical use of available production resources is not only demonstrated by insufficient technological progress, decreasing capital productivity, and a related relatively high labor intensity, but also by the relatively high consumption of production resources. In this economic system, the consumption of essential raw materials, fuel, and energy is much higher per unit of production than in capitalist economies. Research conducted in the CSSR in Spring of 1968 clearly demonstrated a disastrous wastage of production resources,[14] in a country which is already incomparably poorer in raw materials than many of the Western industrial states. This wastefulness is still going on today.[15] Analyses published in 1973 by the Economic Institute of the Prague Academy of Sciences indicate that the consumption of steel per comparable production output runs almost twice as high as in all industrialized capitalist countries in the West.[16] Even a country like Sweden with a much more substantial supply of raw materials has a relatively much lower consumption of steel than the CSSR. The other Eastern

European countries are struggling with similar problems because nothing is more severely criticized by their political leaders than the outrageously high and generally still increasing consumption of raw materials in the production process. In the German Democratic Republic, e.g., the consumption of primary energy per unit of production due to outdated installations and technologies is 20 to 30 percent above the corresponding data for West Germany.[17] More specifically, the consumption of rolled steel is higher by about 30 percent than international standard consumption.[18] The substantially higher relative rate of consumption of all production resources (investment, raw material, energy, labor) is typical of the communist economic system and is undeniable proof of a lack of interest in optimal efficiency on behalf of the production collective and, above all, of the leading economic bureaucracy. The absence of competitive pressure and of market prices as well as the fact that the bureaucracy's income is not tied to market results leads to an attitude of indifference regarding economic effectivity.[19] Individual production decisions are not objectively revised, and the constant moralistic exhortations by political leaders have no impact whatsoever on these countries' economic development. Furthermore, since the planned and controlled productivity of an enterprise is measured by dividing its output by the number of employees, these are even interested in a production development where the registered output is inflated by the highest possible input. With the same purpose in mind, the enterprise manipulates its internal production structure (microstructure). Even reforms such as those introduced in the German Democratic Republic to stimulate the interest in planned profitability have failed to eliminate similar manipulations of production patterns for two reasons: there is no competition and profits can best be increased by manipulating the production structure.

The manipulation of production structures by monopolistic producers leads to great contradictions between the development of the production structure on the one hand, and the demand pattern on the other hand. The result is a permanent and exhausting search for various commodities by all consumers, individuals as well as enterprises in need of raw materials. Although this insolvable contradiction that results in a kind of wartime economy has been verbally criticized for decades, there has so far been no change. While completely unnecessary and unwanted goods are being produced just because their production makes it easier to fulfill the plan, there is a constant lack of other, urgently needed items. Unwanted goods are registered as unnaturally growing stocks representing unimaginable economic losses.[21] If to these stocks is added the already huge and still growing number of unfinished buildings that have been started out of similar planning considerations on the part of the construction industry [22] and absorb a considerable percentage of the national income,[23] the increasing economic losses reflect a production anarchy that by far exceeds the so-called production anarchy of capitalist economies.

However, whereas in a capitalist economy structural disproportions find their expression in periodic economic crises as soon as they reach certain dimensions—since no capitalist businessman can finance the long-term production of commodities that do not sell sufficiently well—the enormous disproportions existing in the communist economies are financially covered by the state. When an enterprise has fulfilled its highly aggregated overall production plan, whose internal microstructure cannot be centrally planned and controlled, it receives the wages in the planned amounts. Its entire production is absorbed by other production enterprises or by trade organizations whether or not there is a current demand for this kind of goods. Demand being at all times higher than supply, every enterprise tries to stock up even on products not actually needed, because this very product might not be available again for the next few months or years. In this way the consumers and not the producers are accumulating reserve supplies that have to be covered by growing state credits. In the meantime, production goes on, with no bureaucratic central organism being able to change this pattern.

As early as 1924, economists such as the Trotskyite R. N. Kricman have criticized the resulting economic anarchy, calling this phenomenon an anarchy of supply. "Thus, in the known proletarian barter society, distribution is organized but supply is not organized. The resulting anarchy is an anarchy of supply."[24] According to Kricman, in a capitalist economy there is always a more rapid increase of demand rather than of supply because the distribution of products takes place in a market anarchy. In the "proletarian" economy, demand is greater than supply because although the distribution of goods is state-organized, centralized production planning does not correspond to real needs and is therefore anarchistic supply planning. While Kricman still believed that it was possible to organize better and more detailed centralized planning of supplies corresponding to concrete needs, it has been admitted later, and is accepted today, that such a detailed plan is not conceivable in view of the enormous variety of different products, not even with the help of the most modern computer systems. But because the bureaucracy, for the sake of its own power interests, is not willing to grant a certain degree of economic independence to the individual enterprise management and because it opposes the introduction of a regulated market and instead holds on to an entirely bureaucratic overall plan without market criteria and market responsibility by the individual enterprise, the supply anarchy with all its devastating consequences for the population has survived until this day.

To sum up, it can be said that the Soviet bureaucratic economic system is incapable of achieving a more efficient development of productive resources than the capitalist system. It lacks the economic incentives, criteria, and mechanisms that in a highly industrialized society ensure a constant adaptation of the supply structure to the demand structure, as well as the most economical use of all potential production resources and a fast technological and qualitative production development. It is the reason why this system will not be able to provide the working population with a higher standard of living. Even countries like the CSSR that had been highly industrialized in the past are now lagging far behind the capitalist states in consumption development instead of surpassing these countries.[25]

Significantly, the propaganda machine only mentions the "great achievements in production growth," carefully concealing any indication of how much higher the level of consumption could be if all the economic losses would be avoided and if instead of pushing for a wasteful, mostly extensive production increase a more efficient production growth had been promoted.

EXPLOITATION OF THE WORKERS

The second characteristic feature of socialist development according to Marx and Engels was the elimination of "capitalist exploitation." The appropriation of the surplus value (surplus of the newly created labor value over and above the value of the productive work force) by private owners of capital was to be replaced by direct socialist distribution of the newly created value.[26] Of course, the elimination of the capitalist trait of surplus labor and of surplus value could not mean the elimination of surplus labor as such, insofar as in socialism, too, the producing workers have to create a surplus product, that is, they have to produce more than what they directly need for current production and for personal subsistence.

Capitalist surplus value, therefore, is only a specific historical form of the socially necessary surplus product without which even the socialist society could not do.[27] This fact has to be underlined for the benefit of all those "Marxists" who isolate the category of surplus value from its general historical context and consequently are no longer able to take a critical look at the surplus product in present-day bureaucratic "socialism." In other words, they need to examine what this surplus product has in common with the capitalist surplus value, and if indeed it is radically different in the sense that one can talk about an elimination of the exploitation of the producing individual.[28]

With the introduction of state ownership of the means of production, private capitalist appropriation of surplus value is no longer an issue. This does not mean, however, that there is a genuinely socialist distribution of the created value, that the surplus value is actually used to benefit the producing individual and in favor of socially required purposes, and that the exploitation of the workers in the sense of the capitalists' appropriation and use of the surplus value has indeed been eliminated. When in a capitalist system the state becomes the owner of the means of production, exploitation according to Engels continues because the workers continue to be wage earners who have no say in the use of the surplus value.[29] But what is the situation in a bureaucratic state?

We have to insist above all on the fact that Marx and Engels always had in mind the systematic elimination of the state after a relatively short postrevolutionary period of transition during which the socialization of the means of production was to be achieved. The state as an estranged institution of power with its bureaucratic apparatus, its police force, prisons, and other repressive instruments was to gradually wither away and be replaced by a common administration of public affairs.[30] This theory is also expressed in Marx's concept that the future distribution of the social product in a socialist society should cover general administrative expenses that are not part of production, but with the provision that "this part will be substantially reduced from what it is in present society and will decrease even further as the new society develops."[31]

However, this very expectation never materialized. In all Eastern European countries the state apparatus instead of being reduced in size is actually expanding more each year—in complete contrast to the expected "withering away of the state." As indicated above on the basis of Soviet sources, the bureaucratic apparatus grows at a faster rate than production.[32] These data are a rarity even though they refer only to the economic apparatus; as for the actual political and administrative apparatus, there are no data available at all. Therefore, it can only be affirmed by the author on the basis of years of personal experience that the entire bureaucratic apparatus grows faster than the volume of productive, cultural, and sociomedical activities. The fastest-growing apparatus are those of the police, state security, and the military. Obviously, the party apparatus grows at the same rate as the entire administrative and repressive apparatus in order to ensure the "leading role of the party."

The huge bureaucratic apparatus that has no comparable counterpart in the Western industrial states is entirely financed by the surplus product. Because all data relating to size and cost of this apparatus are classified, and because instead of controlling and evaluating its activities the population is totally dominated and suppressed by this administration, the use of the surplus product for this purpose can only be called an appropriation by other interests than the working people and, therefore, according to Engels, has to be considered continued *exploitation*. For this very reason, the Marxist definition of "surplus value" is never statistically accounted for in the Eastern European countries. This would be easy to do but is obviously not in the interest of the bureaucracy. Not only is the size of the surplus product a well-kept secret but all detailed data concerning the distribution and use of the national income are concealed as much as possible.

After many years of keeping all data on national income an absolute secret, communist administrations began to publish selected information in the 1960s, but in such an irrelevant context that the people who create these values for society hardly know anything about the size and use of the surplus product. Attempts by a number of antibureaucratic economists to evaluate the surplus product in various "socialist" countries despite the confusion created by biased statistics have resulted nevertheless in the certainty that it is larger than the surplus value in most capitalist countries.[33] Research done by the Czech economist J. Krejci and reported in my book *The Third Way* shows that the growth rate of the surplus value (or surplus product) is higher in the CSSR, Hungary, and Poland than in comparable Western countries such as France, Austria, and Norway. By no means can these findings be interpreted as signifying that the productive individuals in the Eastern European countries receive a larger share of the surplus product than those in the Western industrial countries.

Since many of the Western industrial states have some kind of health insurance and old-age pension plans for wage earners that are quantitatively as well as qualitatively comparable if not superior to the insurance schemes in the Eastern European countries,[34] the relatively higher surplus product in these countries cannot be explained by these kinds of expenditures. In some of the Western capitalist countries, comparable state expenditures for social security are even substantially higher than in Eastern European countries, e.g., in West Germany. Table 2 shows social security expenditures by the following countries in 1969, covering (a) old-age pensions, disability benefits, accident and survivors' insurance; (b) cash payments by health insurance organisms; (c) war pensions; (d) other.

TABLE 2: Social Security Expenditures for 1969

	German Democratic Republic	CSSR	West Germany
Expenditures for social security—social income[1]	12.1 billion M	38.9 billion[3] Kč	78.0 billion DM
National income[2]	107.2 billion M	294.0 billion Kč	443.5 billion DM
Social product in percent of national income	11.3	13.2	17.6

SOURCES:

[1]"DDR Wirtschaft" (Frankfurt, 1971), p. 322.

[2]Data for West Germany converted according to East European methods of processing; see also "Sozialprodukt in Ost und West" in *Vierteljahresbericht zur Wirtschaftsforschung 1973.*

[3]See also *Statisticka rozenka 1972*, p. 540.

Public expenditures for education are probably higher in the "socialist" countries for children of workers and other socially disadvantaged families because for them education is completely free and scholarships are readily available, ensuring students an adequate living standard during college years. However, neither the percentage of educational expenditures taken from the GNP, nor the percentage taken from the country's economic budget are substantially higher in Eastern Europe than in Western industrial countries.[35] In these countries, therefore, overall education is not longer on the average than in the Western industrial countries.[36] It follows that the existence of a higher surplus product in the Eastern European countries cannot be explained by these expenditures either. Also, in the case of the Western countries, we have to add the cost of education incurred by bourgeois families, basically those whose children do not get free education and scholarships. This reduces the differential in educational expenditures even further. If we tried to explain the difference between the surplus product in the "socialist" countries and the capitalist surplus value by educational expenditures in favor of the workers, this would only apply to a very insignificant percentage of the surplus product and thus give no indication as to the real nature of the surplus product.

Apart from the disproportionally high costs of the bureaucratic apparatus, we have to deduct the investment expenditures from the surplus product. However, as explained above, the relatively high accumulation fund is not an indication of "socialist benefits" but is, on the contrary, the inevitable result of, first, slow technological progress and decreasing capital productivity that leads to a situation where lack of quality in capital goods has to be made up for by quantity; second, of the enormous losses due to waste of material, inadequate production structure, unsellable commodities or products undersold in the foreign market, unfinished constructions, and so forth, all of which represent an insufficient national income in relation to accumulation requirements; and third, of the uneconomical production structure that favors the investment-intensive heavy industry. This, in turn, results from the uneconomical use and considerable waste of raw materials, semifinished hardware, energy, and so forth caused by the disproportionate extension of heavy industries, including the steadily accelerated military production sector.

Therefore, the uneconomical growth of the accumulation rate is not explained exclusively, or mainly, by military production requirements, as dogmatic communist ideologues keep insisting with the implication that "it is forced on the socialist countries from abroad." Without dwelling on the complex issue of the political aspect of the arms race, let us just say that capitalist countries, too, have to provide for defense. But although in some capitalist countries such as the United States military expenditures absorb a considerable share of the national income, these countries do not have such a substantial accumulation rate as the Eastern European countries.[37] In fact, capitalist economies simply cannot afford these kinds of economic losses and wastage and the related accumulation rates.

The development of "socialist" accumulation benefits the population only marginally and leads to decreasing consumption. Communist arguments that capitalist accumulation serves to increase private capital do not impress the workers in Eastern Europe at all, for they are aware of the fact that an increase in state capital does not bring any benefits for them. But it does reduce their consumption because of the tremendous inefficiency of the system and the power interests of the ruling bureaucracy.

The workers are fully aware of the losses that are due to the system of bureaucratic economy and of the impact on their standard of living. The steadily increasing stock of unwanted products, the growing number of unfinished buildings, the misinvestments, and increasing state subsidies for financing losses in production as well as in foreign trade all are financed by the surplus product, which instead of being directly beneficial to the workers has thus become a financial means to making up for inefficient bureaucratic organization and management. In 1973, the Czech government had to pay 4.8 billion Kc in subsidies just for covering losses incurred by the foreign trade organisms.[38]

People in the Eastern European countries feel that their labor is being exploited even though they are not able to express and compute this fact theoretically. All they know is that their real wages and the overall quality of life are far inferior to that of the Western countries, and that consequently the highly publicized "elimination of exploitation" has brought no advantages to the workers. They know from their own experience how many hours are wasted in the production process because of irregular supplies and frequent interruptions, and how the plan's quotas are fulfilled by means of overtime work, "storming," and special brigades. For the workers, "planning" is identical with bureaucratic irresponsibility, which they have no power to change since they have no control or decision in the nature and use of their labor's results.

In view of the waste of the surplus product caused by the ruling bureaucracy it is hardly surprising that the leadership is not interested in publicly accounting for the use of the surplus product. It would all too clearly demonstrate that in Eastern Europe the exploitation of the productive individual is at least as flagrant, if not more, as in many capitalist states. For this very reason the bureaucratic leadership is strongly opposed to a more democratic planning, to alternative plans established by democratically elected representatives of the people, and to the involvement of democratically elected organisms in deciding on the allocation of the national product for investments or for satisfaction of the population's various needs.

Only in the case of alternative plans can representatives of the people genuinely participate in decisions on future developments. When a bureaucratic planning organism sets up one single plan that none of the members of the party's Central Committee can understand, not to mention assess, so that this plan has to be accepted as such by the Committee without one single essential modification, and when such a formal act is performed exclusively by the Central Committee of a monopolistic party without a chance of examining alternatives in the framework of free, democratic discussions, then the present system has to be considered a bureaucratic decision-making process involving the creation and use of the national income and of the surplus product, and we have to talk about a *process of exploitation.* Consequently, private-capitalist exploitation as criticized by the classics of Marxism has been replaced by state-bureaucratic exploitation and can by no means be considered a socialist liberation of labor.

ALIENATION OF MAN

Another essential concern on the part of Marx and Engels was to overcome the alienation of the individual caused by capitalist society. The elimination of this negative trait was to be a characteristic of socialist society. But this socialist trait cannot be found in the present Soviet system either. There are various forms and stages of human alienation, and the contention that alienation can be overcome with one stroke by means of revolutionary social changes has to be dismissed as being unrealistic.[39] Besides, the question remains whether it will be possible at all to eliminate forever the symptom of alienation. However, this is not to say that this most essential demand made on socialist society should be brushed aside as a "philosophical issue" and be totally ignored.

Alienation at work, as caused by a highly developed division of labor, probably cannot be eliminated at the present stage of development. Also, many basic human needs are not yet adequately met, and in many developing countries even hunger is impossible to eliminate. Even though it means tying down for a lifetime a great number of people to monotonous and soul-killing activities, there has to be division of labor in order to avoid a decline in labor productivity, because otherwise hunger would become an even greater problem than it currently is. But there are many and differing attempts being made in this direction. Job rotation among the workers of an autonomous work group in view of job enlargement and job enrichment is an experiment[40] that should be supported, developed, and extended.

However, this kind of experiment did not evolve in the "socialist" countries, for what matters here is not the individual and how to lighten his work load, but the fulfillment of the plan. Although there are occasional drives for improving the place of work to make it more healthy and attractive, production targets set by the plan still have priority. The Stakhanov workers, socialist workers' brigades, and competition organizations all serve only one purpose: to increase production by means of overtime work and work records, to give an incentive to other workers to achieve similar results. This is interpreted as the expression of the workers' socialist consciousness. However, hardly any communist politician has ever reflected upon the fact that the increase in production is due to intensification of labor while on the other hand vast amounts of money are lost through bad bureaucratic planning and management.

Even though much more can be done to eliminate an all too rigid division of labor, we have probably not yet reached the stage of development where major differences between jobs as to their creativity and attractiveness could be eliminated or, at least, reduced. Therefore, it is hardly possible to make the elimination of the resulting job alienation a current political goal.

But the need to overcome *man's alienation from society's decision-making process* has been growing steadily. At the present stage of development of productive forces and in view of the resulting dangers for the human environment and the possibilities of worldwide catastrophes, a solution to this situation has to be the essential requirement of any social reform. However, in this very respect "socialist" society has not only become guilty of neglect but has actually greatly contributed to man's further alienation. The population at large has not been asked to participate in social decision making; quite on the contrary, all aspects of decision making in the areas of economics, politics, education, information, and so forth become even less familiar and less accessible.

Means of production, enterprises, production itself, and its results evolve according to decisions in which the workers have hardly any say at all. They cannot implement changes in the modes of production, investment, and distribution; they cannot influence personnel policies; they cannot even fight decisions directly affecting their own wages. The workers are aware of their powerlessness and have become accommodated to their totally estranged environment in their own fashion. Since real wages are low and the bureaucratized enterprises cannot be considered their own, the workers have learned to help themselves. They have organized the theft of material, tools, and products from their place of work. Also, they spend as little energy as possible on the job in order to be able to "moonlight" after working hours with the help of "organized" material. People are happy to hire and even overpay "moonlighters" since the greatest shortages occur in services and especially in the communal repair shops.

Thus, illicit work became very much a way of life, and theft of "foreign" property part of the workers' general "code of conduct." In the commercial enterprises, employees at all levels participate in "under-the-counter" allocations of goods that are in short supply and do not shy away from embezzlement. Despite the threat of severe punishment when discovered, these and similar methods of "do-it-yourself" help are on the increase as a spontaneous reaction to bureaucratic nonsense and mismanagement.

In the service sectors where there is nothing to steal, corruption is in full swing. Medical doctors in the public health services are customarily bribed to avoid long waiting lines and bureaucratized "assembly-line" treatment. In the colleges, too, corruption is well established, with parents trying to get their sons and daughters enrolled despite certain "cadre regulations," or to influence the results of entrance examinations. This abuse has spread to high schools and graduation examinations. In public administration, bribes are common practice, and for the small bureaucrat they constitute a necessary compensation for the high costs of repairs, spare parts, and goods that are in short supply. As for the party functionaries, they use their "connections" with the directors of production and trade enterprises whom they have placed, or helped stay, in these positions, with the difference, however, that this is not called corruption but patronage.[41]

This development certainly has nothing to do with the highly praised "moral unity" of the citizens of the communist states. It cannot be eliminated by education or agitprop, for it is a human reaction to a political and economic situation that, though criticized during decades, has not improved but worsened in its contradictions and shortages. What we have here is the expression of the man in the street's increasing alienation from institutions and organisms, of fear and alienation in the relationships between people, of human self-alienation. Growing material needs, interest in personal advantages, and striving for short-term enrichment increase proportionally to economic shortages, social disillusionment, and loss of ideals and perspectives. The insane ambition of the party ideologues to change human interests by means of propaganda and agitation[42] is in direct contradiction to the basic tenets of Marxism, according to which man is mainly a product of his social environment. But since the party ideologues are incapable of admitting to the system's contradictions, they have no choice but to keep trying to "reeducate" the individual. The absurdity of this bureaucratic activity is clearly demonstrated by the fact that the managers of the propaganda machine themselves do not believe in its reeducational powers.

The reaction is predictable when people have experienced that those who criticize the system in the best intention to change it for the better are silenced, and that it is the less-qualified and most opportunist individuals who make a political career. Part of the population will accommodate, will cooperate, and try to cope as best they can. Those not interested in a political career will use their contacts to ensure a more comfortable life. And those who have no connections will try to satisfy their personal needs by means of illicit work or trade, or by accepting bribes. The other part of the population whose education and ideals do not allow for this kind of accommodation with the system will retire from any form of public life and try to survive in a closed social environment. This, in fact, characterizes the life-style of the majority of the people in "socialism": they live within the circle of family and friends, indifferent to, or contemptuous of, public and political life. This explains the Eastern Europeans' exaggerated drive for the possession of weekend houses, which more often than not are simple wooden sheds somewhere in the countryside. After five days of somehow coping with their job, the workers have two days of respite to be enjoyed away from the place of work in order to be able to face the next five days at the job.

People have to live no matter how well they like the system, how indifferent they feel about it, or how much they hate it. It is possible to forget about the system one doesn't want but cannot abolish by concentrating on one's personal interests and pleasures in life, which always and everywhere has enabled human beings to endure suffering. Some people work in their garden, play cards, or collect stamps. Some get drunk or go hungry while saving up for 15 years to buy an automobile. Some spend their money on food or cook fancy dishes for a hobby. The only times they must think about the system are when they have to stand in line for every piece of meat they buy, when there is still another shortage of vegetables and fruit, when they have to sit for hours in the district physician's overcrowded waiting room, when they have to wait for several months to get that bag of cement, when they have to line up at three o'clock in the morning for spare car parts and still don't get them, when the store is out of the kind of nails they need, when bathroom tissue is available only twice a year, when they want this item, when they need that product. . . .

However, these daily encounters with the "system" have become so much part of everyday life that people have become used to them. "It is no use to get mad if things cannot be changed and, anyhow, life is short enough. . . ." Thus, the drive for consumption, the chase after Western commodities and fashion gear, the eating and drinking bouts become expressions of human alienation just as they have been, and are, in capitalist systems. People are no longer aware of this kind of alienation, and their only regret is that consumption meets with more difficulties in the East than it does in the West. They even have illusions about Westerners' opportunities for unlimited consumption that the communist regimes try to dispel in vain, since the bureaucrats themselves are mainly interested in their own material well-being. On the contrary, the drive to consume is being systematically promoted since people who are interested in consumption represent less of a political threat to these regimes.

Obviously, rage, resistance, and organized opposition are on the increase in this segment of the population and are always latently present. The relation of indifference and rage, resignation and opposition indicates not only a further differentiation within this segment of the population but also a constantly fluctuating behavioral pattern within the individual. A person who today does not want to hear of anything and concentrates on gardening may, at the slightest indication of possible success, tomorrow turn into an active fighter for social transformation. There is indeed a very large number of people who have not been won over by the system and who are in opposition to such an extent that the slightest incident will push them all the way to active resistance. The Husak regime cannot really count on 90 percent of the population as being loyal to the system. This has nothing to do with bourgeois or petty-bourgeois origins but it is proof of the antihumanitarian nature of a system that fills with disgust not only those who are protective of their own "ego," but also those who have recognized that they could have a better life were it not for senseless bureaucratism.

However, suppression and persecution are so powerful and ever-present that only a small minority becomes actively involved in political resistance. These people must be morally strong and courageous to join or even organize political resistance in the face of all the repressive methods applied by the system against dissidents and opponents. The better known a dissident is to the public, especially abroad, and the more support he gets from public opinion, the less likely he is silenced or eliminated by the regime. Whatever the dissident's personal social concept or motivation, his fight will always be a heroic and progressive fight in the sense that he tackles the bureaucratic dictatorship on the issue of the liberation of the individual.

How ridiculous is the term "opportunist" used by the bureaucrats for the Czech reformers when everyone knows the word to describe a person who unscrupulously takes advantage of opportunities or circumstances for his personal gain. The entire Czech population today applies this term only to those politicians and bureaucrats who were afraid to lose their positions during the "Prague Spring" and who therefore contacted their anxious counterparts in neighboring countries in order to prepare the brutal suppression of the reform movement. Do these politicians really expect to eradicate people's personal experience by means of lies and propaganda? Nothing is stronger than personal experience which marks a person, and one of these everyday experiences in the socialist countries is the contradiction between the words of the politicians and the realities of life, experiences that are not forgotten but accumulate in people's memories.

Many people cannot cope with this contradiction and become desperate, especially those who once were full of enthusiasm and expectations and then suddenly, shocked by reality, disillusioned and without ideals, can see no longer any sense in life.[43] The self-alienation of the individual, his feelings of loneliness, anxiety, despair, and disgust have traditionally led to alcoholism and suicidal tendencies. For Marx, suicide was the ultimate expression of human alienation caused by society.[44] It certainly is a symptom originating in various interacting factors and processes. And still, the decisive influence of society, its internal insolvable conflicts, and its unbearable strain on sensitive individuals cannot be overlooked. Marx justifiably accused the capitalist system, but the fact that "socialist" conditions not only accentuate human alienation but also lead to an increase in suicide is one of the major accusations that have to be leveled against this system.[45]

It is no coincidence that it was in the "socialist" countries with markedly "Western" life-styles, such as Hungary, East Germany, and Czechoslovakia, that the people's resistance against Stalinist communism had to be broken with the help of Soviet tanks. The more or less obvious submission of these countries under Soviet neoimperialism has caused great despair and loss of orientation in large segments of the population, and it is in these countries that the suicide rate is the highest and even higher than in all the capitalist countries. Whatever other factors may have contributed, the impact of specific societal and system-inherent factors can hardly be overlooked and should give some food for thought to Marxist theoreticians.

It is inevitable that an unprecedented alienation results from a system that suddenly presses the majority of a country's people into following new directions and adopting totally different standards and goals in contradiction to its previous education, interests, and life-styles, and does not give the people the opportunity of expressing themselves freely and of cooperating in decisions on these new conditions and goals. A political bureaucracy pretends to know what is best for the people and what life should be like in order to meet their interests, while at the same time secretly and brutally pursuing its own specific power interests, which necessarily are in conflict with those of the rest of the population. Such a system is bound to arouse the growing hatred of the majority of the people.

The high-level bureaucrats only meet in their own restricted circles, are only concerned about the interests, needs, and power fluctuations in the political leadership. Since the man in the street has never told them his real opinions, these functionaries are completely isolated from the soul and the consciousness of the people. They will therefore never be able to understand the working man's feelings and will only rule by means of power. The system of absolute bureaucratization has become a system of absolute human alienation.

STATE MONOPOLIZATION AND SOCIAL RESISTANCE

A societal order that is not capable of achieving a development of productive forces more efficient than that of the current capitalist system and therefore cannot ensure the workers a higher standard of living, that has not eliminated exploitation but only modified its form, and that has led to greater human alienation than any of the preceding social orders cannot be a genuinely *socialist* order. There is no sign of the fundamental characteristics as established by the founders of the so-called scientific socialism on the basis of the visions that socialist thinkers during many centuries have had of an overall liberation of man. Even though the official party ideologues loudly proclaim the contrary, they cannot refute the basic criticism of this societal order. There is ample proof of this in the fact alone that they do not dare publish in their very own publications and media the opinions of dissenting socialists and that they have to protect their own contentions by heavy censuring and at the exclusion of discussions.

In this state-monopolistic system power is in the hands of a historically evolved, specific political bureaucracy that is far removed from the people and is motivated by the pursuit of its own power interests, that is, the internal and external consolidation of its position of power. It exploits and suppresses the population and maintains economic conditions that increasingly hamper a potentially efficient development of the country's productive forces as well as a faster rise of the people's standard of living. An organized public brainwashing unprecedented in history takes place by means of biased information, censuring, monopolization of education, science, and art as well as by the state-organized promotion of a dogmatic ideology that has become a new religion. Economically, this power is based on the state-monopolized appropriation and exploitation of all means of production and distribution of goods, with the state as intermediary completely dominated by the party bureaucracy, without any possibility of control or objection on the part of the nonbureaucratic segment of the population.

In the 1960s, M. Djilas became well-known as a critic of the communist system when he characterized the party bureaucracy as the "new class."[46] The ensuing discussion among Marxists essentially centered on his use of the traditional Marxist definition of the term "class." Generally unknown was the fact that the Italian B. Rizzi had already described Soviet bureaucracy as a "class," as A. Carlo recalled in his work. Carlo supports Rizzi's theory of a bureaucrat class in the Soviet Union on the ground that the ownership of the means of production is in the hands of the bureaucracy.[47] This is a remarkable argumentation that can be largely supported by facts.

Without getting involved in lengthy philosophical discussions on this issue it should be mentioned that the main question is whether the Marxist definition of a "class"[48] actually correctly and totally covers all the characteristic traits of this concept, and whether this definition can be accepted as such or has to be completed or modified. It is basically correct to define the party bureaucracy in a communist system as a new class if the constitutionally guaranteed "leading role of the Communist Party" is understood not only formally, but as a de facto monopolized power controlling the means of production, labor, and the production results, and if this exclusive right to control in the economic and political spheres by a separate social group is accepted in philosophical discussion as a generally applied characteristic trait of a class.[49]

Mandel[50] argued that Soviet bureaucracy cannot be considered a class since its removal from power would not result in a different mode of production if a socialist system was to be maintained. This is an unconvincing argument based on an insufficient analysis of the Soviet communist system that for Mandel is a socialist system with a bureaucratic flaw. Also, his contention that it is "the first time in history that a class was established only after it seized power" cannot change the situation in the USSR. First, there are records of social systems whose ruling class did not exist as a class in the previous society, i.e., the class of slave owners. Second, even if such a historic precedent did not exist, it would not change the fact that the political bureaucracy becomes the ruling class only under circumstances that allow for its exclusive control of the means of production, the production process, and the production results under rigidly enforced exclusion of any participation on the part of other classes or segments of the population. The existence and rule of this specific bureaucratic class can be ended only if power is taken from this class by popular uprising, and if the system is largely democratized by introducing a democratic process of decision making in all political and economic matters on the basis of collective ownership of the means of production. These would be the conditions of a genuinely socialist development in the communist countries of Eastern Europe.

The fact that the general philosophical issue of the concept of "class" cannot be resolved in the framework of this book does not change the reality of a party bureaucracy that became the ruling class in a state-monopolized system and whose specific and exclusive interests determine the entire range of political and economic activities of the state. These bureaucratic power interests and antidemocratic goals are manifest in Soviet foreign policy in the form of a new imperialism.

The complex issue of Eastern European foreign policy had to be neglected here since it would require a detailed analysis of international relations and their development as well as the Soviet impact on these relations. Such an analysis would go beyond the possibilities and the framework of this book. However, it is necessary to briefly confirm, and comment on, the validity of Lenin's theory that foreign and domestic policy are always interrelated, and that imperialism goes hand in hand with suppression of democracy.[51] In the same way that the bureaucracy in the Soviet Union ignores the real needs and interests of the population by suppressing all democratic conditions, it acts in its international relations, namely, as an imperialist superpower. All aspects of Soviet behavior toward other nations, capitalist or socialist, are exclusively determined by considerations concerning the consolidation of the Soviet regime, the increase of Soviet direct or indirect influence in the world, and the strengthening of Soviet government and party dominance with other Communist Parties and states. In accordance with these goals, all kinds of imperialist methods are systematically applied, such as direct and brutal subjection, or indirect control of the politics of other states by means of economic influence, threat of armed intervention, and so forth.

Obviously, the Soviet power bureaucracy will always justify even a clearly offensive use of force against other states with the need to protect vital Soviet interests, or to forestall attacks against socialism in other communist countries. But these justifications involving the safeguard of national interests, the necessity to defend the country by preventive actions, and so forth are well-known tools from the imperialist arsenal and can no longer cover up the real motives for these actions, namely, the expansion of power. The Soviet bureaucracy has never voluntarily respected the interests and ideals of other peoples and nations when these were in contradiction to Soviet goals and claims of hegemony. In cases where the Soviet Union could not use force, it has applied the most stringent economic and political sanctions against governments that refused to submit to its rule. But whenever the international power structure allowed for use of force, the Soviet Union has not hesitated to suppress other nations with brutal force as long as this course seemed to serve its interests best.

What a farce the Soviet bureaucrats' imperialist policy has made of the rights of other nations in socialism, rights that had been theoretically declared by Lenin himself: "Victorious socialism must establish full democracy, therefore recognize not only complete equality of rights for all nations in general but also equality of rights as regards statehood, i.e., the right of nations to self-determination, to secession." Political parties that are not willing to recognize such freedom of nations would, according to Lenin, "commit treason against socialism."[52] This is exactly the kind of treason that the present Great Russian bureaucracy is committing by suppressing many nations' rights to freedom and self-determination.

The Czech reformers did not advocate at the time that Czechoslovakia break away from its alliance with the Soviet Union and the other communist states, or that it leave the Warsaw Pact. They only demanded equality within all international organizations as well as nonintervention in their country's socialist development. But the possibility of the Czech antibureaucratic attitude spreading to neighboring Communist countries and the fact that the bureaucracies in these countries felt threatened by a democratic movement were sufficient reasons for brutally crashing with tanks the Czech experiment that was of such great significance to the entire socialist world. Only bureaucrats can proceed in such a way because they are greatly indifferent to a socialist consciousness in their people and could care less about the harm such an intervention will do to this consciousness in the world at large, and because they only rely on their own military force. The result is an increased fight for freedom by the oppressed nations within the Soviet sphere of influence.

Furthermore, all the so-called peace actions and initiatives at the international level are organized by the bureaucratic Soviet regime in the interest of its own political goals as are the "moral" exhortations at home. In the same way the bureaucracy does not care about what the people really think when encouraged to increase production—what counts is the number of "moral" exhortations and mobilization itself—it is not relevant at the international level if there are changes in the attitudes and the relationships between people of different countries and of differing social systems. What counts is to give the appearance of peaceful activity in the hope of reaping specific economic benefits for the Soviet Union. "Peaceful steps" may suddenly be changed into military steps if this seems to be the more likely means of increasing Soviet power and influence, without a thought for the lives of the people involved.

Despite the self-description of "socialist," the bureaucratic system has nothing to do with socialism. To grant the bureaucratic communist ideologues the claim to the only valid definition of a socialist society would indeed mean to make the term "socialism" a synonym of bondage, suppression, and backwardness. The system that has evolved in the Soviet Union, and under its dominance in a number of smaller countries, can only be characterized as a state-capitalist or, more precisely, state-monopolistic and absolutistic-bureaucratized system. The unmasking of the antisocialist and antihumanitarian features of this system, however, does not automatically imply an approval and defense of the capitalist system. On the contrary, the description of the Soviet communist system as state-monopolistic only expresses the fact that the negative traits of capitalism are maximized in the so-called "socialist" system: growing disinterest of the working population in optimal economic efficiency, blatant exploitation by the state, and increasing alienation of the individual. The unmasking of the state-monopolistic nature of the system is the condition for the struggle conducted from socialist positions and aimed at the system's transformation into a *democratic, humanitarian, genuinely socialist* system. The scarecrow of "anticommunism" set up by the bureaucracy cannot and should not stop the fight against the bureaucratic perversion of the great historical ideal of a free socialist society. Only such a fight can make socialism come true.

The fight against the perversion of socialism has to be a fight against the recognized causes of bureaucratic perversion, as the Czech reformers had done in full awareness of this fact. The bureaucratization of the economy will be overcome only by introducing the *internal antibureaucratic factor* in the state-monopolistic countries, in the sense that enterprises become independent and collectively owned and are forced to develop their activities in the areas of management, investment, and production as effectively as possible within the limits of a regulated market. The political rule of the bureaucracy will be ended only by introducing the *external antibureaucratic factor* in these countries, in the sense of democratizing politics and macroeconomic planning on a pluralistic basis.

Socialist democratization presupposes the elimination of the shortcomings and inequalities typical of bourgeois democracy that result from the exclusive ownership of capital by a privileged minority. No separate interest group, and therefore not a bureaucracy either, is to have any special rights allowing this group to impose its specific interests on the majority of the population. This entails primarily the acceptance and institutionalization of certain principles: pluralistic interest groups and organizations, free discussions by means of independent mass media, combined self-government and popular representation, collective capital owner-ship by the entire work force of an enterprise, majority decisions, respect of the rights of minorities, the elimination of professional politicians, direct plebiscites on constitutional issues, the possibility to elect and dismiss leading officials, guaranteed free publications also for minority groups, alternative macroeconomic plans prepared by commissions representing pluralistic interests, popular discussions on the subject of alternative plans in the framework of political election campaigns, independent interest-research institutes closely cooperating with the mass media, partly state-subsidized financing of diversified mass media, as well as numerous other or similar processes designed to promote democracy.

Sooner or later the struggle for this kind of democratization and for the elimination of the bureaucratic rule will gain dimension and strength in all the Eastern European countries, for pressure invariably invites counterpressure even though this process may take relatively longer in some countries, such as the Soviet Union, that have never experienced real democratic conditions. However, even in the Soviet Union the population's growing desire for democratic conditions and for more individual freedom already manifests itself in the dissident movement which is essentially sustained by the technical-economical as well as scientific-cultural intelligentsia. The growing class of young technicians, engineers, business administrators, and so forth and also qualified and progressive workers are increasingly aware of the conflict between their socialist consciousness and the actual Soviet system.[53] These people are in a position to directly assess all the contradictions and losses, and the inflexibility inherent in the system. They see more and more clearly that minor improvements do not make much sense. The apparent contradiction existing between official propaganda on the one hand, and their own personal experience on the other hand turns them into increasingly determined champions for democracy and for fundamental reforms.[54]

Throughout history, the fight against absolutism and despotism has always been initiated by intellectuals. But they have never acted without a social basis. As soon as their voices were heard, one could be sure that their thoughts and demands were understood and supported by the people. This gave them the necessary moral strength to confront totalitarian rule. Without popular support, the Czech reformers would not have been able to conduct their struggle.

Obviously, the attitude of the party bureaucracy is never completely unanimous because great difficulties and increasing dissatisfaction in the population lead to differentiation within the party bureaucracy. Although all bureaucrats agree on the fact that the one-party system has to be maintained and strengthened by means of the "leading role of the party," that is, of the party apparatus, there are, of course, different opinions on the best way to maintain and strengthen the political power of the party bureaucracy.

One segment of the party bureaucracy is especially reactionary in its attitude, believing that power—"socialism" in the official language—can only be safeguarded by maintaining, and even reinforcing, the repressive system. This "Stalinist" faction will always try to explain the system's shortcomings as "remnants of capitalism," instigated by the "enemies of socialism" within the country or abroad. By artificially creating internal and external enemies, the Stalinists hope, first, to divert the population's attention from the system's shortcomings and the bureaucratic causes, and, second, to arouse nationalistic feelings in the population and thus stimulate a wish to maintain the present system. These forces are convinced that in order to cope with all kinds of popular doubt, criticism, and opposition it is necessary to maintain internal and external tension and to create a sort of fighting psychosis directed at the alleged enemies of socialism.

In foreign policy matters, the neo-Stalinists are quite critical of Brezhnev's attitude vis-à-vis the West, especially regarding economic cooperation and cultural exchanges. They advocate the unity of the Eastern bloc and stronger actions against the so-called "revisionists," alluding to Yugoslavia's autonomist regime as well as to progressive tendencies in some Western European Communist Parties.[55]

Another segment within the party bureaucracy is convinced that the system can only be secured if the population enjoyed a higher standard of living and thus felt less motivated to go into opposition. These people will periodically flirt with partial reforms in the hope of increasing economic efficiency and consumption. But since these reforms must not impinge on the nature of the system, which is to say, on the absolutistic rule of the party apparatus, they will not eliminate the main cause of the total bureaucratization of all decision-making processes. However, these relatively liberal bureaucrats are willing to compromise in areas that promise a more speedy rise of the people's standard of living by promoting more active relations with the capitalist countries, by advocating partial reforms in the planning and control system, by reducing censorship in the cultural and artistic areas, and so forth.[56]

These two factions within the party leadership may take turns at being predominant during various stages of development, each time initiating differing political lines and tactics. Each stage will be marked by a few changes in the appartus' personnel structure. But the distinguishing line between the two tendencies will be very subtle and vague, and for the party bureaucrats the fact of belonging to this or that faction is not a question of principle but most likely one of power politics and personal connections. Even though the liberal faction always creates more favorable conditions for serious reform and liberation movements, it essentially remains an integral part of the party bureaucracy. It would therefore be illusionary to expect this faction to eliminate the real causes of bureaucratic despotism. However, the real democrats who try to reform the system will more successfully fight for democratization in a relatively liberal atmosphere than under Stalinist conditions, as demonstrated by the Czech reformers. But sooner or later they will have to face resistance on the part of the entire party bureaucracy, and they will overcome this resistance only with the help of sufficient pressure by the population and by the international community.

Despite the overwhelming power concentrated in the hands of the party bureaucracy and, more precisely, because of this concentration of power, chances of overcoming this power in a foreseeable future are on the rise in all communist countries and especially in the Soviet Union itself. An analysis of the bureaucratized, state-monopolistic economy demonstates its increasing inefficiency, the enormous losses involved, and its incapability of improving the country's standard of living at a faster pace. People who are able to reflect on this situation are not won over by the system, but are repulsed in ever-increasing numbers and are made to think in terms of reforming the system. Growing dissatisfaction and more or less openly practiced opposition by larger segments of the population are reflected in a steadily growing polarization within the party bureaucracy itself. The possibility of an increasingly Stalinist-oriented political development cannot be totally excluded, but at the same time there is justified hope for a strengthening of the more liberal wing within the bureaucracy. In the final analysis, it can be assumed that there are greater chances for a gradual opening of the system for future democratization than for a Stalinist backlash because on a long-term basis pressing interests on the part of the majority of the people will gradually exert influence on the interests of a growing segment of the bureaucracy itself. It is certain that world opinion, too, can and will have a valuable impact on this development.

NOTES

1. See also: Ota Šik, *Plan and Market under Socialism* (New York, 1967), Chap. 1.
2. A. Carlo, ibid., p. 64. "In 1974, the Soviet production growth rate was again

higher in heavy industry than in the consumer goods industry, although the latter was to have priority according to the current five-year plan [ending in late 1975]." *Tagesanzeiger*, Zurich, January 21, 1975.

3. In 1968, Czechoslovakia was, after Portugal, second to last in Europe in housing construction. To this day, the situation has not improved much. On the average, young couples have to wait six to eight years to be allotted an apartment.

4. For more details and concrete facts see Ota Šik, *Für eine Wirtschaft ohne Dogma* [For an economy without dogma] (Munich, 1974); ibid, *Wirtschaft und Gesellschaft im Umbruch* [Economy and society in transition] (Bern, 1975).

5. Vintrova, "Schluesselprobleme langfristiger Prognosen," in *Methodologische Fragen der Prognostizierung der sozial-oekonomischen Entwicklung* [Methodological problems of projecting socioeconomic developments], Institute of Economics CSAV (Prague, 1973), p. 43.

6. J. Zoubek, "East European Economy in 1975," *East-West Research Report*, no. 8 (1975), p. 27; Notkin, "Prognostizierung des Wachstums und der finalen Benutzung des Nationalein-kommens," in Vintrova, *Methodologische Fragen*, p. 19.

7. L. Brezhnev, speech during the elections to the Supreme Soviet, quoted from *Rude Pravo*, June 15, 1974.

8. Ota Šik, *Argumente für den Dritten Weg* (Hamburg, 1973), p. 83.

9. "Soviet per capita consumption is only around one-third that of the United States, about 50 percent that of the United Kingdom, France, and West Germany." From "Economic Aspects of Life in the USSR." Main findings of a colloquium held January 29-31, 1975, in Brussels, NATO-Directorate of Economic Affairs, Brussels, 1975.

10. See data on the trend of the average capital output ratio in Ota Šik, *The Third Way*, p. 299.

11. H. H. Hoehmann, ed., *Die Wirtschaft Osteuropas zu Beginn der 70er Jahre* [Eastern Europe's economy in the early seventies] (Stuttgart, 1972), p. 25.

12. A. Svoboda, in *Rude Pravo*, May 13, 1975.

13. Ota Šik, *Fakten der tschechoslowakischen Wirtschaft* (Vienna, Munich, Zurich, 1969); W. Gatz, ed., *Die wirtschaftliche Entwicklung der BRD und der DDR 1950-1970* [The economic development of West Germany and the GDR between 1950 and 1970] (Bremen, 1974), p. 74.

14. See data in Šik, *Fakten der tschechoslowakischen Wirtschaft* p. 60.

15. See also *Annual Survey of Manufactures 1964-65*.

16. Vintrova, "Schluesselprobleme," p. 45.

17. Hoehmann, *Die Wirtschaft Osteuropas*, p. 68.

18. *Der Spiegel*, no. 41 (October 7, 1974), p. 42.

19. R. Bernheim, *Die sozialistischen Errungenschaften der Sowjetunion* [Socialist achievements in the Soviet Union] (Zurich, 1971), p. 80.

20. L. Strougal, *Hauptrichtungen der Wirtschaftspolitik der Partei in den Jahren 1971-75* [Major trends in the party's economic policy between 1971 and 1975] (Prague, 1971), p. 10.

21. According to *Rude Pravo* of June 26, 1974, the entire volume of stocked products in the CSSR at the end of 1973 had a total value of 230 billion Kč, an increase of 14 billion Kč since 1972. This sum corresponds to about two-thirds of the national income. In Poland, according to *Rude Pravo* of September 24, 1974, the value of stocks amounted to 87 percent of the national income.

22. The volume of unfinished buildings increases because of shortages in secondary supplies (windows, doors, electrical installation, and so forth) but construction goes on to meet the planned targets.

23. In 1973, unfinished construction in the CSSR represented a total value of 220 billion Kc.

24. R. N. Kricman, "Die heldenhafte Periode der grossen russischen Revolution," *Vestnik der kommunistischen Akademie*, no. 9 (Moscow, 1924).

25. J. Hajek, *Demokratisierung oder Demontage?*, p. 92.

26. K. Marx, "Critique of the Gotha Program," *Selected Works*.

27. K. Marx, *Capital*.

28. J. Y. Calvet, "Socialisme? Ou capitalisme a masque humain?" *La Voix Ouvriere*, October 12, 1973. As Marx himself has made sufficiently clear, all social production orders produce a kind of surplus product. The only difference is who appropriates this surplus, and how is it used.

29. F. Engels, *The Development of Socialism from Utopia to Science*.

30. See also Šik, *The Third Way*, chap. 4.

31. Marx, *Critique of the Gotha Program*.

32. See chapter 3.

33. See also Šik, *The Third Way*, chap. 8.

34. In the CSSR, wage earners are entitled to a minimum old-age pension, with the exception of formerly independent craftsmen and peasants even though they may have joined a cooperative in later years. Hundreds of thousands of old people who do not qualify for special bonuses thus receive only the minimum monthly pension of 550 Kč, although the official minimum subsistence level is set at 789 Kč a month. These old people either have to depend on their children, or they have to go back to work.

35. For data on public education expenditures in 1970 see K. von Beyme, *Oekonomie und Politik im Sozialismus* (Munich, 1975).

36. P. Sager, *Die technologische Luecke zwischen Ost und West* [The technology gap between East and West] (Bern, 1971).

Average education in years:	U.S.	11.6
	Northern Europe (West)	9.0
	Soviet Union	6.8
	Italy	5.3
Percentage of college graduates in work force in the mid-1960s:	U.S.	11.6
	Soviet Union	3.8
	Northern Europe (West)	3.2
	Italy	2.6

37. See Table 16, p. 524, in *Statistisches Jahrbuch der Bundesrepublik Deutschland 1972*.

38. *Rude Pravo*, June 26, 1974.

39. Šik, *The Third Way*.

40. Volvo in Sweden, and Norsk-Hydro in Norway. See G. Bihl, *Von der Mitbestimmung zur Selbstbestimmung* [From co-determination to self-determination] (Munich, 1973).

41. In Spring 1975, the First Regional Secretary of the CPC in Pilsen even had to be dismissed because of corruption that had been all too evident in this case.

42. "One of the basic criteria of efficiency in mass political activity and agitation is the increasing coordination of people's individual, collective, and overall social interests." Kase, Director of the Agitation Section of the CC-CPC, as quoted from *Rude Pravo*, June 13, 1975.

43. A. D. Sacharov, *Mein Land und die Welt* [My country and the world] (Vienna, 1975), p. 15.

44. Šik, *The Third Way*.

45. For further details see United Nations, *Demographic Yearbook 1972* (New York, 1973), chapter on General Mortality (Death and Death Rates by Cause, part on Suicide and Self-inflicted Injuries).

46. M. Djilas, *The New Class—An Analysis of the Communist System* (London, 1957).

47. A. Carlo, *Politische und Oekonomische Struktur der UdSSR (1917-1975)* [Political and economic structure of the USSR] (Berlin, 1972), p. 11.

48. V. I. Lenin, "The Great Initiative," *Coll. Works*.

49. Crosland, "Die Zukunft des Sozialismus" [The future of socialism] in *Wohl-fahrtsstaat und Massenloyalitaet* (Welfare state and mass loyalty), eds. W. D. Narr and C. Offe (Cologne, 1975), p. 93.

50. E. Mandel, "Ueber die Buerokratie" [On bureaucracy], *Die Internationale*, no. 2 (Hamburg, 1974), p. 52.

51. V. I. Lenin, "On a Parody of Marxism," *Coll. Works*.

52. V. I. Lenin, "Socialist Revolution and the Right to Self-Determination," *Coll. Works*.

53. V. Belotserkovsky, "Letter to the Future Leaders of the Soviet Union," *Partisan Review*, 42 (New York, 1975), p. 265.

54. Ibid., p. 265.

55. W. Leonhard, *Am Vorabend einer neuen Revolution?* [On the eve of a new revolution?]

56. Ibid., p. 124.

POLITICAL AFTERWORD

This book was written to reveal the truth about the communist power system for all to know. In particular, though, I address myself to those forces in the capitalist countries who see the future of mankind in *socialist transformation*. With the capitalist system's internal contradictions and difficulties increasing, and its capability of mastering the problems of the future without a change in system declining, the responsibility of those who advocate socialist reforms becomes even more evident. We are faced more urgently than ever with the vital question of which route to take and how to direct social thinking in order to arrive at essential solutions. I insist on warning all those who, when looking at Soviet society, are convinced to see socialist transformation in action despite various "initial childhood diseases." Being abstract and theoretical by nature, an analysis cannot possibly convey the extremely frightening process of human deformation realistically enough to shake the reader. It probably takes a very talented and articulate writer to render in detail the moral decline, corruptness, and cynicism so typical of the functionaries and bureaucrats, and the power intrigues, propaganda lies, hypocrisy, ignorance, formalism, and pseudoactivities thriving in the communist system and affecting the entire population. In this respect, the preceding pages are by far not eloquent enough and describe the bureaucratic system's negative tendencies and consequences only in a rather matter-of-fact way.

The highest treason committed against the ideal of socialist liberation of mankind is not the result of "childhood diseases," but of the characteristic features of a bureaucratic system that pretends to be socialist. The system's representatives, who stand and fall with its existence, will keep asserting that all this is not true, and that these allegations are manifestations of "bourgeois anticommunism." Any criticism, as justified as it may be, is dismissed with this convenient slogan. Once more I want to make it very clear that for me the future of mankind lies in a democratic and humane socialism. Terms such as "renegade" and "traitor" that are used to describe me, or the misrepresentation of my real opinions, will not succeed in distorting my socialist conviction and making it appear as "antisocialism."

I am fighting with all my experience and knowledge against the communist perversion of socialism because I want to see socialism come true for the individual, and not for the bureaucratic functionaries. My task today is not only to tell the truth about the communist system but to point out the *causes* that have led to this system's antisocialist perversion. To know the causes is essential not only for changing the present system but also for preventing in the future bureaucratic communist systems from being established in other countries. Anybody who is not only interested in personal power but also genuinely cares about the working people cannot and should not turn away from the effort that it takes to study closely the arguments and facts reported in the preceding analysis, as well as in many other works.

It looks as if in the Communist Parties of Italy, Spain, and other countries new concepts are evolving today on a future socialist development within the framework of pluralistic democracy. It is to be hoped that all Communist Parties recognize the fundamental significance of democratic conditions for genuine socialist progress. However, this must not be understood to mean that they should continue to ignore the repression of democracy in the Eastern European countries and its antisocialist implications. The Western Communist Parties have to assume the historical responsibility of thoroughly examining and *theoretically* applying the Czech analyses and reform models. It is not enough to protest against the occupation of Czechoslovakia, for protest alone does not change the situation of the Czech people. Not only the fact of approving the Czech reform movement, but also the ideological and political consequences from that experiment have become the essential touchstone for the genuineness of humane socialist aspirations. Following the Soviet lead, a number of parties submissive to Moscow denounced the Czech reformers as "traitors against socialism." But what the communist power bureaucrats call treason is the logical separation of the reformers from those who long ago committed treason themselves against socialism. Anyone seriously fighting for the progress of socialism has to take his distance from bureaucrats, careerists, and hypocrites because these people do not represent genuine socialism, which they have discredited in the eyes of the population.

I consider it my duty as a scientist to reveal the true nature of the communist system. This means that I no longer, for some political-tactical reason, try to formulate my observations and opinions in ways that *could* make them acceptable to the communist rulers. In this sense, politics and social sciences have to be kept apart. There is no doubt about the usefulness of political strategy. In the communist countries it always has been, and unfortunately always will be, necessary to phrase a theoretical study in such a way that it is not immediately condemned and suppressed as "anti-Marxist," "hostile," and so forth, even though its author feels much more critical and, under more liberal circumstances, would have used much stronger language. Disguised truth or carefully formulated information can be effective, too. It can be propagated in various ways in the communist countries and may even make a lasting impression in some communist quarters. I myself and the other reformers had to proceed very carefully during many years in order to be able to bring about some changes and to avoid being silenced immediately as "enemies." Those who refuse to understand this kind of tactical approach do not know anything about politics and have not reflected on the possibility of reaching an important goal under the existing circumstances. International politics are made very much along these lines.

However, this must not be understood to mean that one should not see things as they really are in the Eastern European countries, nor that one should have illusions about the nature and development of the communist system. On the contrary, those who do not consider political strategy as self-serving, and who do not want to have to adjust continuously to the existing power structure, who are interested in furthering the liberation of mankind, can not *only* make "realistic" politics. It is possible to compromise to a degree with the adversary one has to live with, provided it helps promote liberalizing measures and changes in favor of an oppressed people. It will be possible only on the basis of long-term political strategies for internal and external adversaries of bureaucratic communist regimes to compromise with the Soviet bureaucratic system and to exploit the arrangement to the advantage of a future democratic and genuinely socialist system. For many years the Czech reformers, fully aware of the real nature of the bureaucratic system, were able to make their tactical moves within the party in view of approaching the main goal, namely, the fundamental reform of the system. But as soon as chances for a reform had been destroyed by military intervention, the reformers had to leave the party. The opportunity for implementing a change of system was lost, and any further cooperation with the reactionary bureaucratized regime would have brought the reformers into disrepute.

Once it has been established as a certainty that the communist system is an antisocialist, state-monopolistic, and bureaucratic system, its transformation into a genuinely socialist system becomes the basic criterion of socialist behavior, even though this goal may be far away. Insofar as strategic steps are made in view of such a transformation, they can be acceptable; under specific circumstances even a "careful" description of the system's features may qualify as such a tactical step. But when a "careful" characterization of the system is used to conceal its true, nonsocialist content and admits only to secondary shortcomings or initial flaws, we have to call it treason against the people's real interests and support for the communist state-monopolistic bureaucrats. The attitude toward the real nature of the system, toward the fight for its socialist transformation, and, consequently, toward the effort of the Czech reformers remains an essential criterion for all sincere socialists.

Those, however, who are indifferent to the ideal of socialism, who oppose a democratic socialist development—because they are conservative proponents of capitalism or simply pragmatists without long-term goals in mind—will be tempted to comply with the Soviet superpower in order to preserve world peace and the capitalist system. This is a justifiable position, although the question remains to be asked if this policy can in fact ensure the long-term capitalist goal. In any case, such a policy will have to be backed up by a systematic deployment of military power.

The same is true for the proponents of a democratic-socialist transformation of the capitalist system who at the same time are determined to prevent a bureaucratic, state-monopolistic totalitarian development in their own countries. As long as there have been no fundamental democratic changes in the Eastern European countries, these forces cannot afford to take a nihilistic stand in the issue of their countries' defense potential. On the contrary, as democratic-socialist changes and greater freedom and social progress for the working people become more of a reality in the West, these countries need an even more efficient defense mechanism against the state bureaucracies of the East. Not to understand this fact means not to understand the antihuman, antidemocratic and neoimperialist character of the Soviet communist system. The more successful the democratic systems are, the higher their standard of living, and the greater their peoples' political freedom becomes, the stronger the incentive will be for the peoples within the communist system to fight for democracy, and the more desperately the reactionary Stalinist factions within the Eastern party bureaucracy will fight for their position of power. But they will secure their power not only by means of increased internal repression, but also by external expansion directed primarily against the seats of infectious democratic development. As long as these Stalinist bureaucratic forces have not been defeated completely by real democratic changes, and as long as the danger of expansionism has not been removed, Western democratic forces cannot give up their military security.

Obviously, further democratic and truly socialist reforms in the West would encourage the fight for democratic freedom in the

Eastern European countries, just as any intensified state-monopolistic and bureaucratic developments and restrictions of democratic forces in the West serve to strengthen the position and the interests of the Stalinist bureaucracy in the East. It becomes more and more evident that the decisive antagonism in world development today exists between two contrasting developments: on the one side, state monopolization and antidemocratic, antihuman bureaucratization resulting in increasing repression of the population. On the other side, a systematic democratization process in the political and economic areas that provides growing opportunities for the people to decide democratically, and without manipulation by specific interest groups, on the country's development, at both the macro- and microlevel of society. The more this process of democratization in the Western states leads to democratic socialism, the more incentive it gives for the fight for democratic freedom in the communist countries. In this regard, the increase of contacts between peoples in the East and peoples in the West, as made possible by dètente, becomes particularly important.

Because détente encourages the liberal forces in the East while limiting opportunities for the Stalinist forces and reducing their potential for starting conflicts and building up enemies, this policy should be supported and promoted by all progressive forces. However, détente must not be based on illusions about the Soviet communist bureaucracy. To the Stalinist forces, which pursue their own goals within the apparatus and the party organs, détente is no more than a temporary strategy serving in the current situation as an adequate means for furthering their politics of hegemony. Considering these Stalinist tendencies, the Western powers should actively pursue their policy of promoting democracy and preventing aggression. The more limited the opportunities are for creating international tension, anarchy, and aggression, and thus for escalating military preparation, the greater the chances are for maintaining peace and promoting worldwide social and democratic progress. By intensifying economic, cultural, and other relations between East and West, and by proceeding more uniformly, carefully, and systematically in this approach, Western democracies can improve the conditions in the fight for freedom by the democratic forces in the East.[1]

However, Western foreign policy has to be well-coordinated and set long-term goals as does Soviet foreign policy—which has not given up on its efforts to extend its hegemonic, Soviet communist influence in the world, despite détente. Since a democratization of the system in the Eastern European countries is also one of the essential conditions for eliminating its neoimperialist character, the long-term goal of Western foreign policy should be the *real democratization in the communist countries*. Even if such systematic Western foreign policy cannot forestall *definitely* a possible renaissance of Stalinist tendencies in the Soviet Union, a possibility that cannot be discounted totally, it offers nevertheless *greater chances* for democratic liberalization in the Eastern European countries than a Cold War policy, which may lead eventually to a world catastrophe.

The complicated issue of international relations cannot be analyzed in greater detail in this context, but it had to be mentioned at least in order to reach a better understanding of the differentiation in the social development of the Eastern European countries. It is hoped that this analysis of the Soviet communist system will stimulate the socialist forces in the West to become once more seriously interested in the real meaning of socialism.

The fact that a large segment of the working population in the capitalist countries is still afraid today of socialist changes is mainly due to those Communist Parties that, after having seized power, have established a state-monopolistic instead of a socialist system. Bourgeois propaganda would never be able to conceal or distort indefinitely the advantages of a socialist system if these advantages really existed. Those holding the mirror to communism are not responsible for blocking the road to a socialist future, but those who are afraid to look into this mirror. Criticism cannot be brushed aside indefinitely by slander and insult, but it will grow and become a strong political force, as long as bureaucratic communism represses the people. Only by undergoing change will the communist system be able to stop theoretical reflections by its critics.

NOTE

1. See also Ota Šik, "Die politische Bedeutung der Ost-West-Wirtschafts-beziehungen" [The political significance of East-West economic relations], in *Für eine Wirtschaft ohne Dogma*, pp. 74-87.

INDEX

ABOUT THE AUTHOR

OTA ŠIK, born in 1919 in Pilsen, Czechoslovakia, was deputy prime minister under Dubček until August 1968 and one of the leaders responsible for the "Prague Spring." A professor of economics and reputed theoretician, he now teaches at St. Gallen University in Switzerland. His other works include *The Third Way—Marxist-Leninist Theory and Modern Industrial Society* and *Arguments for the Third Way*.